L. L. Bean Fly-Fishing Handbook

Written and Illustrated by
DAVE WHITLOCK

NICK LYONS BOOKS
WINCHESTER PRESS

Produced by
NICK LYONS BOOKS
212 Fifth Avenue
New York, NY 10010

Published and distributed by
WINCHESTER PRESS
New Century Publishers, Inc.
220 Old New Brunswick Road
Piscataway, NJ 08854

PRINTED IN THE UNITED STATES OF AMERICA
10 9 8 7 6 5 4 3 2 1

Designed by Susan Newman
All the casting photographs in this book were taken by Lefty Kreh.

First trade edition, 1984.

Library of Congress Cataloging in Publication Data

Whitlock, Dave.
  L.L. Bean fly-fishing handbook.

  "Nick Lyons books."
  Bibliography: p.
  1. Fly fishing—Handbooks, manuals, etc. I. Title.
II. Title: LL Bean fly-fishing handbook.
SH456.W45 1983   799.1'2   83-25893
ISBN 0-8329-0301-9

Contents

The Joys of Fly Fishing

One afternoon last summer, Dave Whitlock and I fly-fished up a little feeder creek in Yellowstone Park. It was a warm afternoon and we were in no particular hurry—which is the best way to fish—so we fished together and then alone, and we talked a lot, and we caught a few trout. Dave did most of the catching.

The particular brand of fly-fishing we did was unusual and I had not done it before. Big fish had come up into this feeder stream from a larger, famous river whose temperature got quite high in August. The fish, Dave told me, were in the stream for relief from the heat, not food. You had to tempt them with a fly they could not refuse. He suggested a grasshopper, which is a mouthful, and he gave me a new version of his famous Dave's Hopper. Dave is one of America's most innovative fly tiers and—had I been a trout, and as they proved—this fly looked good enough to eat.

Dave showed me how to approach a bend pool, how to stand fifteen feet back from the bank, how to cast so that merely the leader fell on the water. These were special techniques, local refinements. He gently corrected a hitch or two in my casting and helped me perfect a knot—for he is a deft instructor.

About five o'clock, beneath a stand of lodgepole pine, we picked some small wild strawberries, sat on the mossy ground, looked up at a singularly blue sky, talked about the fish we'd seen and caught, compared notes. We were both smiling broadly at the exquisite pleasure of the past few hours. He said he wished everyone had a chance to spend at least one afternoon like this—back in wild country, with a good friend, learning a new technique or two, fly-fishing to difficult

trout, catching a few. Fly-fishing was at the heart of it.
Twenty years earlier, I said, before I fly-fished, the
day would have been impossible. The particular peace
and pleasure I felt were intricately connected to the
brand of fishing I practiced—the rhythmic cast, with
rod and line becoming extensions of my arm; the
subtle drop of the fly, which imitated a natural insect;
the intimate knowledge of the stream and our quarry
that we needed to fish this way. And I was still learning. That was part of fly-fishing, too: it became more
and more fascinating and (no matter how good you
got) there was always something new to learn. The
afternoon had been a blend of satisfactions: skills
already mastered and new skills that I had learned—
none of them difficult to learn, though once I'd
thought so.

We used equipment that was balanced and under-
stood. Line, reel, and rod were matched, and could
do our bidding. The simple and lovely act of casting a
fly—in this case one tied by Dave—was in itself
rewarding. We had to stalk the fish, in gorgeous surroundings, and we had to know why they were here
and on what they might feed. You could not merely
chuck out a bait or lure and chance a fish coming by.
We had to "read" the water, know our fish, actively
hunt them. We were more closely connected to the
subtle web of nature than we could possibly have
been through any other pastime I could imagine. We
were more *involved*—physically and mentally—than
had we practiced any other fishing method. The wild
strawberries we ate—which were soft, bright crim-
son, astonishingly sweet—were only the most palp-
able symbol of our connection with the natural world.

Dave and I were ourselves an example of the magic
fly-fishing weaves. He lives in Arkansas and I in a
large eastern city; for him, fly-fishing is a way of life, a
consummate art to be practiced with cunning and
increasing skill; for me it is that, too, but also a respite
from the work and tension of cities: as the modern
world has become more and more mechanized,
crowded, even harsh in its metropolitan pressures, I
have grown to love fly-fishing the more and to appre-
ciate its gifts, for itself and as a sorely needed tonic. It
demands such happy skill of hand and eye, knowledge

of the fish's world, imagination; it always challenges and refreshes me. Dave and I were from sharply different worlds—rural and urban—and may even have fly-fished for different reasons; but we shared an absolute joy in this special art of angling. Fly-fishing had brought us together, taught us a common language, made us friends.

Too many people avoid fly-fishing because they think it is too difficult to learn. Some take it up without proper instruction and then drop it. This little handbook is an antidote. It has one simple purpose: to be a clear and eminently practical introduction to the sport. It seeks to take the mystery out of fly-fishing and to make it accessible to a vast number of people who might otherwise avoid the sport.

To my mind, this handbook does the job with unique skill. That's not surprising. For the past five years, Dave has been working with L.L. Bean to develop the L.L. Bean Fly-Fishing Schools. It has been a happy and successful venture. With the company's encouragement and support, Dave has developed a variety of new teaching techniques and methods; he has refined his own considerable skills as an instructor; and he has found the simplest and most effective ways to get people started fly-fishing. Since his methods worked so well with hundreds of students, L.L. Bean thought they ought to be in print; the result, I think, is like spending a weekend fishing with Dave.

Dave will introduce you to fly tackle, fly-casting, fishing tactics, fly tying, and other tools and skills that will make this sport of limitless interest to you, regardless of your age, sex, income, or athletic ability. You will learn that it is *not* beyond your ability to cast well and with accuracy, and that with a little patience and practice you can tie your own flies—and then catch fish on them—and that this will double your fly-fishing pleasure. Dave will surprise you by showing how many different species can be caught on a fly—not only trout but also bluegill, bass, bluefish, on up to sailfish and even marlin; fly-fishing can be practiced not only in rivers but also in ponds, lakes, estuaries, and the ocean. Since Dave is a skilled artist, he has supported his text with a multitude of helpful line drawings and charts. In all, this book can provide the down-to-earth basic instruction you need to get you catching fish on a fly.

Then, once you've learned the fundamentals, you will want to go on and learn more—for fly-fishing can become a finely tuned art. And in a short time you'll know why millions of fishermen consider fly-fishing the most versatile and challenging—as well as the most enjoyable—way to sport-fish. As my afternoon with Dave on that haunting western stream reminded me: it is also a singularly compelling way to enjoy the outdoors.

—NICK LYONS

Photo by Darrel M

1
Understanding Fly Tackle

Fly-fishing is a purely manual method of sport-fishing that involves the casting, presentation, and manipulation of an artificial fly to hook, play, and land fish. Fly-fishing is unique because the tackle components—rod, reel, line, leader, and fly—are used differently from the ways tackle is used in such other popular angling methods as spin-casting, spinning, and bait-casting. In fly-fishing, you use the fly rod to cast a hand-held, weighted line that propels an almost weightless lure (the fly) to the fishing area. Other methods employ a weighted lure to pull an almost weightless line off a reel.

Fly rod and reel are designed to control and cast the uniquely shaped and weighted fly line. Fly rods are generally longer and suppler than other rods, to allow optimum performance in casting, presentation, and fly and line manipulation. The fly reel does not function during casting and fishing the fly. It holds excess

In conventional casting (called bait casting or plug casting), the rod motion (A1) sends into motion a weighty object (A3), which pulls the line out. But in fly casting, the rod motion (B1) casts the fly line (B2), which pulls the fly out after it.

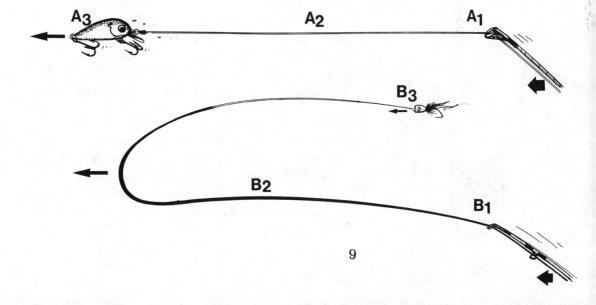

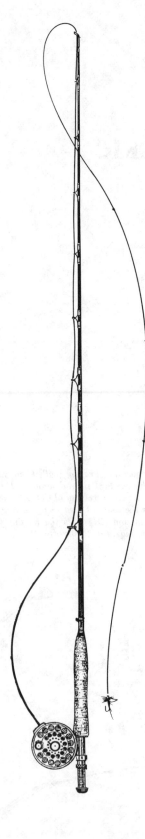

fly line (and backing line) during casting and fishing and acts as a line-extending or -retrieving winch once a fish is hooked. The leader, a light, nearly invisible extension of the heavy, highly visible fly line, aids in presenting and manipulating the fly.

Flies, which may imitate any type of natural fish food (such as insects, minnows, shrimp, or frogs), are cast near the fish with the fly rod and line. The feel and control you receive from the hand-held rod and line during all the fishing activities make fly-fishing the most pleasurable and stimulating angling method.

This seemingly handicapping manual method actually has nearly limitless possibilities—far more than other methods that use artificial lures. This potential will become apparent once you get started in the sport.

There are five tackle components essential to fly-fishing: line, leader, rod, reel, and fly. Fly tackle—the tools or equipment of the sport—work together most efficiently when they are balanced, or matched, to one another. Thanks to a commitment by fly-tackle manufacturers, most components are coded with the information needed to guide you in assembling a balanced outfit.

The Fly Line

The fly line is the key component of the fly-tackle system. The fly line appears to the user of other casting methods to be unusually thick; this is because weight and taper are built into a fly line to aid in casting and in making the line float or sink. Line diameter does not necessarily correspond to line weight, as is true of lines used for other angling methods. Fly-line sizes are standardized, calibrated according to a code adopted by the American Fishing Tackle Manufacturers Association (AFTMA). There are 21 sizes, or weights, of fly lines in this coding system. They are measured in grain-weight units from 60 to 850 grains. An AFTMA fly-line size is calculated by weighing the first 30 feet of line (excluding the tapered tip of the line). However, ten line weights (3 through 12) cover most needs of the fly fisher. The three most popular line weights are 6, 7, and 8.

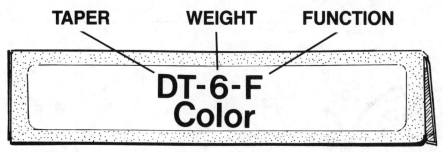

TAPER   WEIGHT   FUNCTION

DT-6-F
Color

The AFTMA Fly Line Code.

All modern fly lines are clearly marked and coded on their containers with the AFTMA line weight and other simple design and use codes. The design and weight of a fly line determine how the fly is cast and presented to the target. Just as importantly, design and weight can also determine the depth at which the fly is fished.

The modern fly line is constructed with a central core of level braided nylon or similar synthetic material. The core provides strength, part of the line's weight, and the foundation for layers of coating. The coating generally consists of one or more layers of a molded plastic or vinyl material and provides the line with a durable shape (or taper), most of its weight and flexibility, its density, and its color. The coating also has a very smooth, nearly frictionless surface for line movement through the rod's guides, your hands, and the water.

Composition of a modern fly line: A. Braided nylon core. B. Plastic coating with bubbles or lead powder. C. Coating varies to provide proper casting weight. D. Core is level through length of fly line.

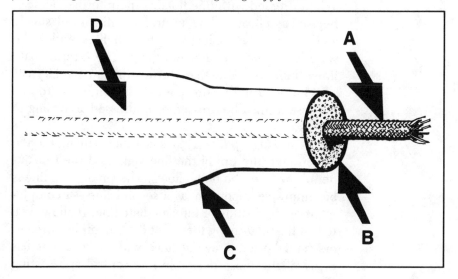

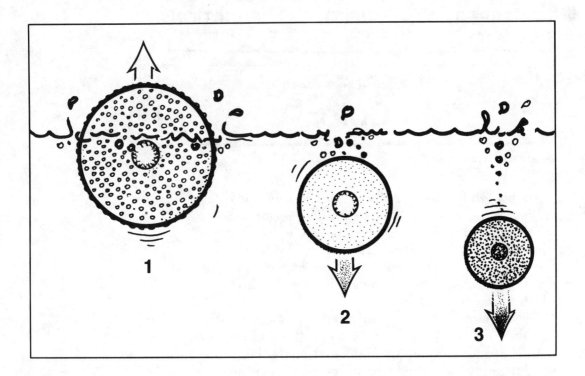

Cross-sections of Three Line Densities of
Same Weight
1. Floating fly line. 2. Intermediate.
3. Fast-sinking.

The *floating line* (F) is buoyant to ride on top of the water. It is used primarily when fishing dry flies (floating flies), but it may be used with wet flies, streamers, or nymphs (sinking flies) in shallow depths of streams and lakes.

The *intermediate line* (I) is slightly heavier than water, and it is sometimes referred to as a neutral-density line. Most of the old silk-core fly lines were neutral in density. The modern intermediate fly line, with a nylon core, is becoming popular as a dual-purpose line—a floating line and a slow-sinking line. When dressed with line flotant, the intermediate can be used as a floating line; undressed, it will sink slowly and can be used effectively to fish flies under the water's surface, but not too deep. The intermediate line is more practical than the floating line, and it casts a bit better. But the intermediate is a bit more trouble because it must be dressed or undressed according to the use.

The *sinking-tip line* (F/S) is just that: The first ten to fifteen feet (the tip) of the line sinks and the remainder of the line (the belly) floats. The sinking-tip line is becoming very popular as a second line—a complement to the floating or intermediate line. It allows you to fish floating/diving flies, wet flies, nymphs, streamers, and bottom-crawling flies with ease, yet it has many of the more desirable line-control and casting characteristics of a floating line. It is much easier for beginners to use than a full-sinking line. It is excellent for fishing flies at depths of 2 to 10 feet.

There are several tip-density choices with sinking-tip fly lines, which allow sinking speeds of slow, medium, or fast. The faster-sinking (or higher-density) tips keep the fly deeper while it is being retrieved or while it is drifting in a stream's current.

The *sinking line* (S) is used to pull a fly down to a depth of from a few feet to as much as 30 feet in streams, lakes, and salt water. Sinking lines are useful for standard casting and retrieving techniques as well as for trolling. They are made in different densities to allow you a choice of sinking rates from slow to very fast. Most of the density variation is created by impregnating the fly line's coating with lead powder.

The three main fly-line styles—floating, intermediate, and sinking—in the same AFTMA line weight will have different diameters. The floating line will have the largest, the sinking line the smallest. The line diameters differ because all must weigh the same. The thicker floating line will *feel* lighter than the same weight sinking line, and it will not cast quite as far with an equal amount of effort. This happens simply because the floating line's greater surface area creates more drag on the rod's guides and in the air.

All fly lines are made in one of three shapes: level, double taper, or weight forward. Each design has casting characteristics that you should understand in order to choose the right line for your needs. Although a fly line is more complex in make-up and higher in price than monofilament spinning line or braided bait-casting or trolling line, with proper care it will last considerably longer than these other lines.

The *level line* (L) has a level braided core and a level molded coating throughout its length. It works well for casting and roll-casting short distances (20 to 40 feet). Because it has so much weight and so great a diameter at the tip end, it limits your ability to make delicate or complex presentations. Generally, we do not recommend using a level fly line to learn proper fly-casting and presentation methods.

The *double-taper line* (DT) is tapered on each end and has a uniform diameter in the midsection. The tapered tip permits more delicate and controlled pre-

Fly-Line Styles

LEVEL

DOUBLE TAPER

WEIGHT FORWARD TAPER

Three fly line designs

sentation of the leader than does the level tip of the level line. The double taper is best suited for most short and medium distance fly-casting and roll-casting. Its larger midsection, however, hinders the shooting of line for distance casting (over 60 feet). The double taper is the most popular line design, and it has the advantage of longer life than the other designs, for it can be reversed on the reel when the front tapered end begins to wear out.

The *weight-forward line* (WF) has a tip taper generally identical to the tip of a double-taper line. It has a short, heavy midsection tapering to a long, lighter, level shooting section. The weight-forward line casts well at all distances. Roll-casting distance, however, is limited to approximately 40 feet. Beyond that distance, the smaller shooting-line section reduces roll-casting efficiency. Although it cannot be reversed for longer life as the double taper can, the weight-forward line is the most versatile line design.

There are two important modifications of the weight-forward taper: the bug taper and the saltwater taper. Both are designed to cast larger, heavier, more wind-resistant leaders and flies or to cast such flies and leaders under windy conditions. These lines have a short, blunt tip taper, a heavy and short head, or midsection, and a long shooting section.

One other fly-line design is the *shooting-head line* (SH). This is a special-purpose modification of the double-taper or level line. To create a shooting-head line, the first 30 feet (the head) of a level or double-taper line is spliced to 100 feet of 20- to 30-pound-test monofilament or a special, very small diameter level

BUG - SALTWATER TAPER

SHOOTING·HEAD TAPER

|← Head →| |← Shooting Line →|

Two fly lines designed for special uses

fly line (the shooting line). The shooting head is for casting long distances (70 to 120 feet) by virtue of the nearly frictionless shooting line. The shooting head, however, is relatively difficult to use and is not a good choice for beginners.

The visibility of the fly line to the angler affects your overall fly-fishing performance and success. White, pastel, or fluorescent lines are easier for the fly fisher to see than dark or neutral colors, such as brown, green, or grey. Thus they allow greater control over casting and fishing the fly. But the lighter colors are more visible to the fish, which increases the chance of scaring the fish. In bright light, a fly line in the air looks larger than it is. And when a fly line is on or beneath the water, the fish may see it as an unnatural object and become frightened. Dark or neutral colors are less visible above or in the water.

We recommend that the beginning fly fisher compromise and choose a highly visible line to enhance the learning of basics in casting, presentation, and fishing techniques.

The size, or weight, of the fly line you choose should be based on the flies you are going to use (hook size, weight, and wind resistance). Generally speaking, the smaller line sizes (3, 4, and 5) are best suited to flies tied on size 8 to 28 hooks. The medium line sizes (6, 7, and 8) are better for size 1/0 to 12 flies. The large line sizes (9, 10, 11, and 12) are better for size 5/0 to 4 flies. Keep in mind that very wind-resistant or heavily weighted flies will require a larger line size than given in the general parameters already mentioned. The line-size choice is determined by the

Visibility

line's ability to control the fly. If the fly controls the line, you will have casting problems.

We recommend the double-taper fly line for learning basic fly-casting and fly-fishing skills. The double taper requires less critical timing, loads the fly rod efficiently for casts of all distances, and presents the fly most easily. It is economical, and it will serve well for advanced casting and fishing techniques, too. Double-taper line weights of 6 or 7 are the most practical for learning—and they are also the most versatile for general freshwater fishing.

The Leader

The leader provides a low-visibility link between the heavy fly-line tip and the fly. Of almost equal importance, the leader should assist the fly line's front taper in casting and presenting the fly and letting the fly float, swim, or sink in the most natural manner. The leader has four parts, which work together to accomplish these functions.

The *butt* section is the largest in diameter, and it resembles the fly-line tip in flexbility and density— continuing the taper of the fly line.

The *body* (midsection) joins to the butt to provide an additional length of low-visibility material to the leader and to continue the taper.

The *tip* joins the tapering midsection with a smaller diameter length of level monofilament. The tip is usually 12 to 24 inches long; this provides the maximum fish-deceiving length while helping to allow a natural movement to the fly in the water. The leader's tip is also referred to as its tippet if no additional length of monofilament is added.

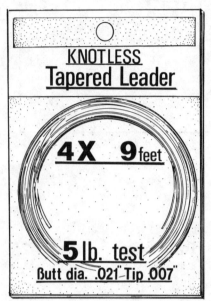

Typical tapered leader package. Identifies leader type, length, size, and pound test of tip.

Knotless tapered leader with parts indicated and tippet attached

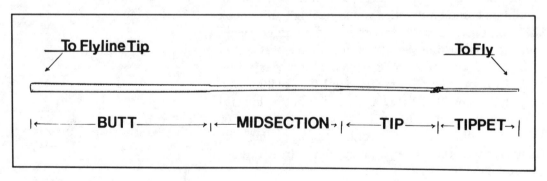

An extension of one or more smaller diameter sections of monofilament tied to the tip of the leader is called the *tippet*. It can be used simply to lengthen the leader, or it can be used to add a smaller-diameter section of monofilament for deceiving fish better. Or the reason for a tippet can be to allow the use of a smaller fly. A tippet may also be added to repair or replace part of the tip. Wind knots often occur in the tip or tippet during the course of a day's fishing, as does abrasion damage or breakage, and these conditions are corrected by cutting out the problem section and replacing it with a new section. The tippet is usually 18 to 24 inches long. Tippet material is sold in convenient, pocket-size spools, individually or in sets, with about 10 to 25 yards of material on each spool. The spools are usually color-coded or otherwise well marked to indicate monofilament diameter and breaking strength. It's a good idea to use tippet material of the same make as the leader.

Typical tippet material spool. Identifies tippet size, diameter strength or pound test, and amount.

Tippet length should be 18 to 24 inches for most uses and flies. Refer to leader-tip/tippet-size/fly-size chart for correct tippet size (diameter and breaking strength).

FLY-LINE, LEADER, AND TIPPET CHART

Type of Fly Line	Leader Length (Feet)	Place to Use
Floating (L, DT, WF)	6 to 7½	Narrow, weedy, brushy creeks and small ponds
	7½ to 9	Most creeks, streams, ponds, and lakes
	9 to 12	Very clear, calm, shallow, slow-moving spring creeks, ponds, and lakes
Floating Bass and Salt Water (WF)	7½ to 9	Most bass, pike, and panfish streams ponds, lakes, and saltwater areas
Sinking Tip (DT, WF)	4 to 6	To fish most waters listed above from 3 to 10 feet deep
Full Sinking (DT, WF, ST)	2 to 6	To fish most waters listed above, 4 to 20 feet deep

LEADER TIPPET AND FLY SIZE
(For optimum casting, presentation, and fishing performance)

Leader Tip or Tippet	X Code	Pound Test	Fly-Hook Sizes
(Diameter in thousandths of an inch)			
.003	8X	1.2	24,26,28,32
.004	7X	2	20,22,24,26
.005	6X	3	16,18,20,22
.006	5X	4	14,16,18
.007	4X	5	12,14,16
.008	3X	6	10,12,14
.009	2X	7	6,8,10
.010	1X	8.5	2,4,6
.011	0X	10	1/0,2,4
.012	X1	12	2/0,1/0,2
.013	X2	14	3/0,2/0,1/0,2
.014	X3	16	5/0,4/0,3/0,2/0
.015	X4	18	6/0,5/0,4/0,3/0

Based on monofilament nylon, Aeon, and L.L. Bean product

Note: This chart is a simple guideline. Fly-hook wire sizes, hook-shank lengths, extra weighting, and material designs, as well as variations in leader-material stiffness, all affect performance. In situations where water is very clear and calm and fish are very selective, longer, smaller-diameter leaders and tippets are more effective because they are less visible and allow the fly to look and act more natural.

A shock, or bite, tippet is a short section (3 to 12 inches long) of very heavy monofilament (20- to 100-pound-test) or metal wire that is added at the fly to prevent fish with sharp teeth or body parts from cutting off the fly. A shock tippet is used for such species as sharks, barracuda, muskellunge, and pike.

There are two types of leaders: the compound knotted leader, and the knotless leader. The compound knotted leader is made by tying together sections of nylon monofilament of different diameters to create a desired taper and length of leader. The knotless leader is a continuous length of tapered monofilament. We strongly recommend the knotless leader for most fly-fishing, because it has greater freedom from tangles, snags, and knot failure.

Leaders are manufactured in 6-, 7½-, 9-, and 12-foot lengths. The longer leaders—the 7½-, 9-, and 12-foot lengths—are generally used with floating lines. The 7½-foot leader is good for very narrow streams, for waters with a rough surface, or murky water. The 9-foot length is best for general conditions. The 12½-foot length is best for clear water with a very calm surface. For sinking-tip and full-sinking fly lines, 7½-

foot and 6-foot lengths—and even leaders as short as 2 feet—are useful. The shorter the leader, the more effective is the sinking portion of the line in getting the fly to the desired depth.

Backing

Backing line is a braided nylon or Dacron (12- or 28-pound test) added to the back end of the fly line. The purpose of backing is to add extra line in case a fish is strong enough to pull off more than the fly line (a fly line is usually 80 to 120 feet long). Backing also serves to fill the reel spool's excess capacity. This setup allows the reel to retrieve the fly line more efficiently and also allows the fly line to be stored on the reel in relatively large coils. These large coils make straightening the fly line easier, and a straight, coilless fly line casts and fishes better. Monofilament nylon should never be used for backing, as it will cause tangling and reel-spool damage. The amount of backing used is dictated by the reel-spool capacity, the fly-line size, and how far a fish might run when hooked.

The Fly Rod

The traditional symbol of the sport, the long, slender, and graceful fly rod, is secondary to the fly line in importance. The responsive fly rod gives you the control and feel that makes casting, fishing, and catching fish on flies so much fun.

The fly rod transfers energy and control from the fly fisher to the line, leader, and fly. Rod length, taper, and action are specifically designed for this purpose. Bait-casting or spinning rods will not perform well for fly-fishing.

The fly rod must be balanced with the correct fly-line weight for optimum performance in fly-casting and presentation. Most fly rods manufactured in the past ten to fifteen years have the correct line-balance information printed on them just forward of the handle and hookkeeper. Usually, the line-weight range is given along with the rod's length and approximate weight.

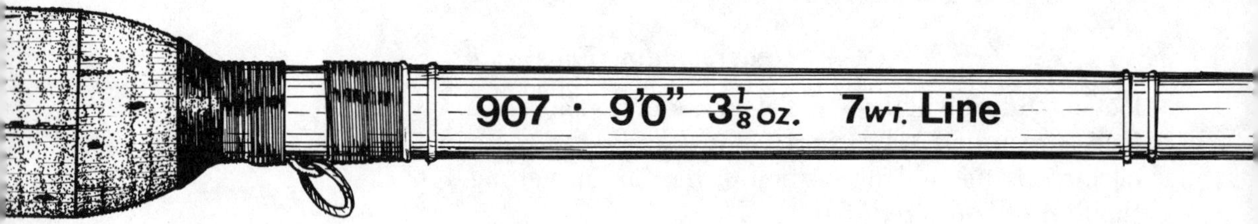
907 · 9'0" 3⅛ oz. 7wt. Line

Specifications listed on fly rod include recommended line weight

The accompanying illustration shows the typical rod-specification markings. Model Code Number 907, 9-foot, 3⅛ ounces, 7-weight line. (Note that the Model Code Number 907 indicates a 9-foot rod for use with a 7-weight line.)

Rod Parts

There are six parts to a fly rod.

The *butt* section, a major part of the rod, includes the area from the handle to the first ferrule.

The *tip*, the other major part of the rod, is the section from the last ferrule to the tip-top, or smallest, guide on the end of the rod. Most rods today are two-piece models. Three-piece rods, of course, have a middle piece, and multipiece rods (such as rods for backpacking anglers) separate into many sections for reduced length when traveling.

The *handle* includes the butt cap, the reel-lock seat for attaching and securing the fly reel in place, the cork grip (also called handle or rod-hand grip), and the handle check cap.

The *hookkeeper* is a ring or other simple device that holds the fly's hook safely in place when the outfit is rigged but the angler is not fishing.

The *guides* hold and control the line on the rod during casting. The guides include the stripper guide (or stripping guide), which is the first guide up the rod from the rod handle and which should be made of a low-friction, hard material. The stripper guide's large inside diameter reduces surface wear between line and guide. The snake guides hold the fly line close to the rod during casting. Snake guides are light and nearly friction-free to allow easy casting and retrieving of line. The tip-top guide holds the fly line at the end of the rod, and, like the other guides, it is designed to be practically friction-free and also to prevent tangling of the line on the end of the rod.

The *ferrule* is the connection between sections of a fly rod. Ferrules are installed so a rod can be disassembled and conveniently carried and stored.

Modern fly rods are made from one of four materials. Each material has different performance char-

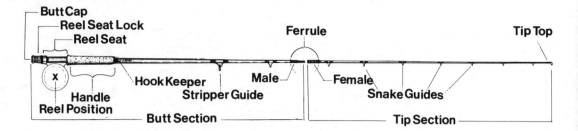

Butt Cap
Reel Seat Lock
Reel Seat
Ferrule
Tip Top
X
Hook Keeper
Male
Female
Handle
Stripper Guide
Snake Guides
Reel Position
Butt Section
Tip Section

acteristics and different production costs. The right fly rod for you depends on the type of fishing you will be doing, your level of skill in fly-fishing, and what you can afford. The four rod materials are bamboo, fiberglass, graphite, and boron.

Today's *bamboo or split-cane rods* are combinations of traditional craftsmanship and modern technology. Those built from high-quality Tonkin cane are lovely to look at and can be very enjoyable to fish with. They are, however, expensive and require considerable care. Smaller sizes may be particularly fragile; larger sizes can be quite heavy and tiring to use.

Fiberglass rods are a fine choice for an angler's first fly rod. They are the least expensive, they are durable, and they are good for most types of fly-fishing.

Graphite or carbon-graphite rods are relatively new, but they have had a significant impact on fly-rod selection. Carbon-graphite is a synthetic fiber introduced by the aerospace industry. Graphite rods are lighter, more powerful, more sensitive, and more efficient than similar fiberglass rods. A well-designed and constructed graphite rod is an excellent fly-casting and fishing rod for fly fishers at all levels of experience. Some graphite rods are reinforced on the outside with fiberglass.

Boron rods are the newest on the market. Boron is a synthetic fiber with high-performance fly-casting and fishing characteristics. Practical rods are made from it today, and the material holds greater promise for the future.

Rod Materials

Detail of guide types on fly rod

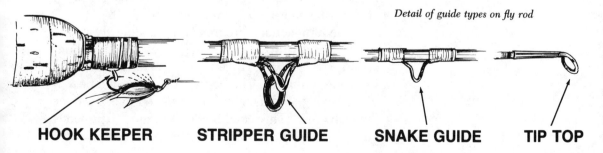

HOOK KEEPER **STRIPPER GUIDE** **SNAKE GUIDE** **TIP TOP**

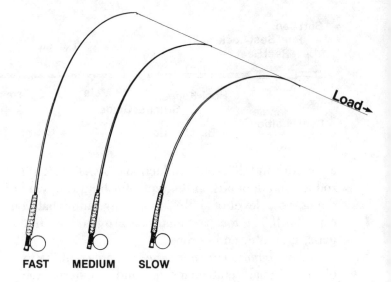

How fly rods of different actions flex under load

FAST   **MEDIUM**   **SLOW**

Rod Action

Fly-rod performance, especially during casting but also while fishing the fly and fighting the fish, is termed the **action** of the rod. Action is influenced by the rod's material, taper design, length, and such fittings as ferrules and guides. There are countless variations in fly-rod actions, but all can be put into three main categories. A fast action is one in which the rod feels stiff when flexed and, when loaded, or flexed by the line in casting, unflexes rapidly. A medium-action rod is limber when flexed and unflexes smoothly when loaded. A slow-action fly rod feels very limber; when it unflexes after loading, it does so in a slow, willowy manner.

Regardless of their action, all fly rods should flex progressively from tip to butt under varying loads. This flex produces excellent performance at casting distances of 20 to 80 feet and casts a wide range of fly sizes and weights. When you are fishing the fly, the tip and butt provide the action. When you are setting the hook on a fish, the tip is the principal energy absorber. The midsection and the butt are the energy transmitters. Once the fish is hooked, the rod becomes a lifting and pulling tool. It also transmits the fish's movements to your hand and absorbs the shock of the fish's more violent movements.

A medium-action, progressively loading fly rod is the best rod with which to learn the sport. Medium action is the most adaptable to a person's individual timing and reflexes. The beginner's rod should be 8 to 8½ feet long, and it should be designed to cast a 6- or 7-weight line. This combination is light, it provides enough power to cast 20 to 60 feet, and it can control most of the flies used to fish for trout, bass, and panfish.

After you begin to master the basic fly-casting strokes, qualified instructors will be able to advise you on which action best suits your own reflexes and coordination level. Generally, the quicker your own reaction time, the faster the rod action that will suit you. A person who tends to be relaxed and to have a smooth, slow reaction is better suited to a medium- or slow-action rod. Once you are properly matched with a rod, your skill as a caster should progress rapidly.

The Fly Reel

The primary function of a fly reel is to contain the backing, the fly line, and the leader. Other functions are to retrieve line and aid in fighting fish. While you are fighting a fish, the reel provides a variable degree of resistance (called drag) that helps tire a strong-swimming fish as it pulls line off the reel. A fly reel, unlike spinning or casting reels, does not perform any casting function.

The reel is positioned and locked onto the fly rod directly behind and under the fly-rod grip. In this position it counterbalances the rod's weight during casting and fishing. There are three basic types of fly reels: the single-action, the multiplier, and the automatic.

The *single-action* reel is a simple direct-drive winch with a one-to-one ratio. One complete revolution of the reel's handle causes the reel spool to make one complete revolution.

A well-designed single-action fly reel should be lightweight and corrosion resistant. It should also have interchangeable spools. The proper size spool should hold the fly-line that matches the rod you intend to use, plus 50 to 100 yards of backing. The reel should have an adjustable drag to prevent line from free-spooling when it is pulled out by the angler or a fish. Another useful component is an exposed, flanged spool for palming or finger-dragging to increase pressure on a running fish. An audible click drag is useful to let you hear how fast a fish is taking

Types of Reels

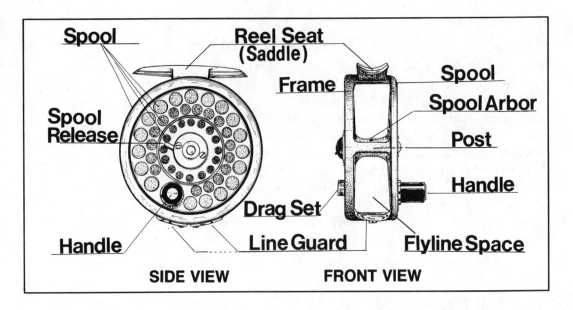

Spool

Reel Seat (Saddle)

Frame

Spool

Spool Arbor

Post

Spool Release

Handle

Handle

Drag Set

Line Guard

Flyline Space

SIDE VIEW   **FRONT VIEW**

The parts of a typical single-action fly reel

line out. A spool with perforated sides is lighter than one with solid sides, and allows wet line to dry when stored on the spool.

The *multiplier* reel is similar in design to a single-action reel, except that it has a complex winch with a one-to-greater-than-one handle-to-spool ratio. One turn of the handle causes the spool to revolve 1½ to 3 times. Such a fly reel is most useful when fast or long line retrieves are routinely necessary.

The *automatic* reel is designed to rewind line automatically. If you have ever used a roller type of pull-down window shade, you know the principle. As fly line is pulled off the reel by the caster, the action puts tension on a built-in coil spring. Then you can quickly and mechanically wind the line back onto the spool by lifting a spool-spring tension lever.

The automatic fly reel has very limited capacity for line and backing and offers no quick-change, extra-spool options. Because of its spring-loading design, it has a very coarse and unadjustable drag system. Only a limited amount of fly line can be directly pulled off the reel without releasing the spring tension. This limitation is troublesome if you need to pull additional line or backing off the reel. The automatic is quite heavy and mechanically unreliable in many fly-fishing situations. It is best suited for fly-fishing where short casting is used, fast retrieves are needed, and the fish does not take line off the reel.

The single-action reel is the most popular and practical choice for most fly fishing. We recommend this type of reel in a size that will hold a 6- or 7-weight fly line and the appropriate amount of backing.

The beginner's outfit we recommend, then, consists of an 8- or 8½-foot fly rod, a 6- or 7-weight line, and a single-action reel of the proper size for the line and backing. We believe this is the best outfit with which to learn the basic skills of fly-fishing.

Flies

The fly is an artificial lure designed either to imitate natural fish foods or to otherwise stimulate a fish into striking. "Fly" doesn't necessarily mean an imitation of an insect, but rather is a term that covers a wide variety of artificial fishing lures.

The fly seldom weighs more than ⅟₃₂-ounce and usually weighs less than ⅟₆₄-ounce. Flies are made of lightweight natural or synthetic materials such as feathers, furs, yarns, latex, plastics, lightweight woods, and threads.

There are four important aspects of artificial flies: size, action, shape, and color.

Size is extremely important—and especially so when the food it imitates is less than an inch long. Action is important, too, for a fly must seem alive or otherwise in a natural state. Shape adds an impressionistic or realistic imitation of the food form. Color enhances the imitation by increasing visual recognition and attracting the fish.

Two types of fly designs are floating (dry) flies and sinking (wet) flies.

The dry, or floating, fly rides on or in the water's surface. Dry flies come in a wide range of sizes, color patterns, and shapes, and they may imitate aquatic or terrestrial insects, small animals, reptiles, amphibians, or even plant seeds.

The floating fly's effectiveness is determined by its shape, the material from which it is made, and how it is manipulated by the angler on the water's surface. The flies listed below can be fished many ways, varying from sitting motionless on the surface to fluttering, wiggling, popping, diving, or skipping across the surface. These actions imitate natural floating foods

Types of Flies

No-Hackle Dry Fly   Hackle Dry Fly   Skater Dry Fly

Floating Nymph

Muddler

Deer-Hair Bug

Typical sinking flies

Wet Fly

Wooly Worm

Soft-Hackle Wet Fly

Nymph

Matuka-Mylar Streamer

and so attract the fish. Floating-fly designs include:

1. Hackled dry flies
2. No-hackle dry flies
3. Bass poppers
4. Hair bugs
5. Muddlers
6. Spiders
7. Skaters
8. Sponge bugs
9. Floating nymphs
10. Terrestrial insects

Wet, or sinking, flies are designed to imitate a wide range of submerged terrestrial or aquatic organisms. Sinking flies may also be designed to stimulate a reflex response that makes a fish strike.

Sinking-fly materials are either water absorbent or heavier than water, so the fly sinks. The fly's shape and density and the fishing method used determine how deep it is fished. Sinking-fly designs include:

1. Traditional wet fly
2. Soft-hackle fly
3. Nymphs
4. Streamers
5. Egg flies
6. Attracters
7. Bucktails
8. Woolly worms
9. Eelworm streamers
10. Leeches
11. Emergers
12. Woolly buggers

Sinking flies are more effective than floating flies overall because most of the time fish feed under the water's surface. Underwater food is more abundant and easier for the fish to detect. Besides, a fish feeding under the surface exposes itself to fewer predators than it does while feeding on the surface.

Floating flies are usually effective during the warmer weather when both terrestrial (land-based) and aquatic (water-based) foods are more active and abundant. Adult aquatic insects (such as mayflies, caddisflies, and midges) and terrestrial insects (such as ants and beetles) are far more active during warmer weather. At times, minnows and aquatic-insect nymphs (immature aquatic insects) will also gather at the water's surface to feed, to flee underwater predators, or to hatch (as in the case of nymphs). During times of such surface activity, floating flies that imitate what are normally subsurface foods are effective.

Eelworm Streamer

Initial Assembly of Fly Tackle

The initial assembly of fly tackle can be confusing to any person new to fly-fishing. This confusion largely results from the components that are closely related to the fly line itself—that is, the reel, backing, leader, and tippet. If possible, seek the help of someone who knows how to assemble fly tackle.

Accompanying diagrams include instructions to give you a clear picture of how to set up the complete tackle system used in most fly-fishing. The instructions are divided into two parts: first the initial assembly, using the fly-rod butt section and other components except rod tip section and fly, and then the assembly for actual fishing.

After removing the fly rod from its protective tube case and cloth case, attach the reel to the reel seat. Make sure that the line guard of the reel is facing forward and that the handle of the reel is on the opposite side of the rod from the hand with which you cast. Usually, we recommend that you cast with your stronger (or master) arm and hand, and retrieve with the other hand. With this arrangement, you do not switch the rod from your stronger hand to your weaker hand when you need to reel in line—as you must do if you elect to place the reel handle on the same side of the rod as your stronger hand. Tighten

The elements that combine to connect fly reel to fly

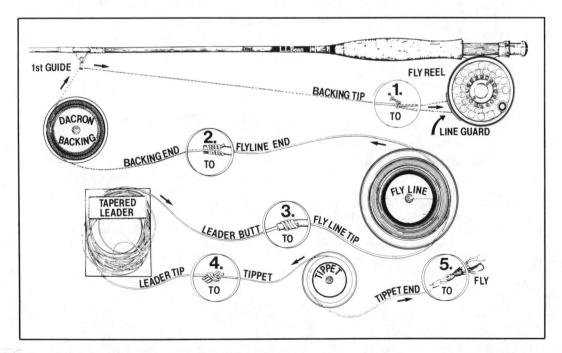

the reel seat so that the reel does not rock from side to side or move forward and back. Use finger pressure only—avoid using a wrench or pliers to tighten the reel seat.

After setting up your tackle for the first time, the next step is to put the backing on the reel. When the reel is mounted on the rod, you can easily reel on backing, line, and leader because the rod provides a convenient handle.

Backing to Fly Reel

First, put a pencil or pen through the hole in the backing's spool. This provides a convenient means of holding the spool. Then take the end of the backing and pass it through the stripper guide (top to bottom) on the fly-rod butt. This arrangement aids in maintaining direction control and drag as you reel on the backing.

Pass the backing end through the reel's line guard, over and around the spool (spindle), and back out the same way. Make sure that you have not looped line around or passed line over one of the reel's frame posts. Now pull off at least 12 inches of line through the reel to accomplish the following steps:

Near the tag end of the braided backing line, tie a simple single overhand knot. Draw it tight, as close to the end as possible. Trim off any tag and excess.

Pass the tag end of the line around the backing that leads to the spool. Now make a second simple overhand knot—this one around the line that leads to the backing spool—and tighten it down. Result: a loose slipknot around the spindle.

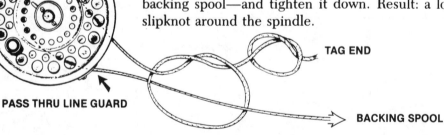

PASS THRU LINE GUARD

TAG END

BACKING SPOOL

1.

BACKING TO FLY REEL

1. Put a pencil or pen through the hole in the backing's spool. Take the end of the backing and pass it through the stripper guide (top to bottom) on the fly-rod butt, then through the reel's line guard, over and around the spool (spindle), and back out the same way. Make sure you have not looped line around or passed line over one of the reel's frame posts. Now pull off at least twelve inches of line through the reel.

2. Near the tag end of the braided backing line, tie a simple single overhand knot. Draw it tight, as close to the end as possible. Trim off any tag and excess.

3. Pass the tag end of the line around the backing that leads to the spool. Now make a second simple overhand knot—this one around the line that leads to the backing spool—and tighten it down. Result: a loose slipknot around the spindle.

The Duncan Loop, described and illustrated later, is an even better knot for attaching backing to reel, especially when fishing for very large fish.

Now pull on the line to tighten the slipknot down around the reel spindle. Erratic pulling will help you slip the knot into place. Ask someone to hold the backing spool with a pencil or pen through the spool hole. Then begin to reel the backing onto the reel. Always wind on line with a forward, down, back, and up motion, clockwise with your right hand or counterclockwise with your left. Use just enough line tension to ensure that the backing is firmly on the spool. Try to position the consecutive windings on the spool evenly, going from right to left and vice versa. Your rod-hand index finger can be used to control tension and level winding as you reel on both backing and fly line. You should fill the spool with backing to the level that allows the right amount of space for the fly line. This is sometimes hard to judge. If you're in doubt, ask someone—a fly-fishing friend or a tackle salesman, for example—how much space to leave for the line size you intend to put on the reel. Some reel manufacturers provide this information.

If no help is available you can determine the proper amount of backing by putting the fly line on first and then the backing over it. Fill the spool to within about one-quarter to three-eighths inch from the top— about the width of your little finger's tip. Mark or cut the backing at that point. Then remove the backing and fly line. Now begin with the backing, attaching it to the reel by the method already recommended.

After putting the proper amount of backing onto the reel spool, you are ready to attach the back end of the fly line to the backing. If the fly line is stored on a spool that has a center hole, put a pencil, pen, or dowel through it to control unwinding. Pull at least 24 inches of backing off the reel spool, and pull the back end of the fly line off its spool. Make sure when using a weight-forward line that you are attaching its proper end to the backing. Most manufacturers mark it in some way. If it is not marked, pull off about 15 feet of line to see if it is the narrow running line or the thick head section. You must attach the tip end of the narrow running line to the backing.

To attach the line to the backing, carefully follow

Fly Line to Backing

the accompanying diagram of the *tube knot*. The tube knot provides the smallest possible connection between line and backing, which reduces the danger of tangling with the line on the spool, the rod guides, or obstacles in the water. You need a one- or two-inch-long metal, wooden, or plastic tube, with a diameter similar to or slightly larger than the fly-line diameter. The braided backing will easily pass through a tube of this diameter. You may also use a needle with a large eye, or a needle of the type used for inflating footballs and basketballs. If you decide to use an inflation needle, you must cut off the tip and smooth the remaining rough edge. Now the needle is open at both ends.

THE TUBE KNOT
(BACKING TO FLY LINE END)

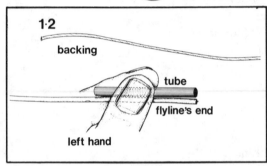

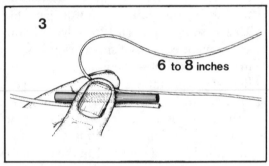

1. First straighten the ends of the braided backing line and the fly-line tip by pulling and stroking each with your hands. If straight, they will be easier to handle while tying the tube knot.

2. Place a two-inch-long hollow tube (about the diameter of the fly-line) and the fly-line tip ends together, parallel in your left-hand thumb and index finger with about 1¾ inches of each past your finger tips to your right.

3. Next place backing end between fingers next to and parallel to fly-line and tube so that end extends past thumb and index finger to your left about six to eight inches. Hold all three firmly.

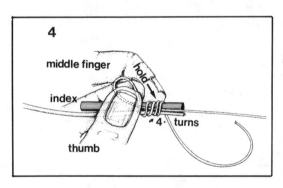

4. With right-hand thumb and index finger grasp backing end and loop the end around, bringing it to the right of your left finger tips. Now wrap it over, behind, and around fly-line tip, tube, and leader section four times. Make each consecutive wrap tight and as close as possible to the other, just in front of finger tips. Use your left middle finger to hold wraps down to prevent them from springing up and forward if wrapping tension is released. Try to keep fingers slightly relaxed to avoid fatigue.

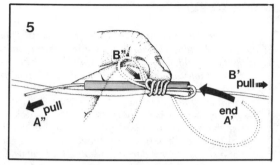

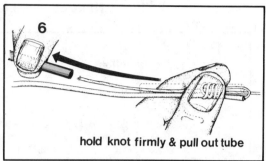

hold knot firmly & pull out tube

5. While firmly holding line, tube, and four backing wraps in your left hand (A') put end of backing into right side of tube and push backing end left, completely through tube. (A") make sure end is completely through tube. With right-hand fingers pull on (B') backing at right until first loop (B") on left side of wraps pulls down next to first four wraps.

6. Now reach behind left-hand fingers with your right and carefully pull tube to the left and out from between left fingers. As tube is removed continue to squeeze fly-line and backing end wraps softly with thumb and index fingers so they will not loosen, misalign, or come apart.

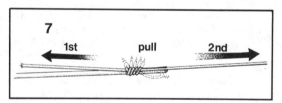

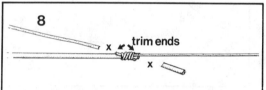

7. With right hand pull first on backing end and second on backing to tighten all knot wraps that are between left hand and thumb and index finger. You should feel the four wraps tighten down. Before final tightening take a peek at wraps and if needed position or align them as in diagram with fingers and finger nails.

Now with fingers firmly pull on both backing sides to tighten knot down on fly-line. Excessive tightening pressure is seldom needed. With too much pressure backing may cut through fly-line coating and cause knot failure.

8. Clip excess backing line end and fly-line tip away with nail clippers or scissors. Give several firm pulls on fly-line and backing to test knot against slippage or failure.

NOTE: Knot can be made a bit more durable and trouble free by one or two coats of flexible fast-drying waterproof nail polish or fly cement. The tube knot may be a faster, simpler substitute for the fly-line/leader (No. 3) needle knot but does not function quite as efficiently as the needle knot.

Now that you have the backing and fly-line on the reel, you should attach the leader. The butt section of the leader is attached to the tip end of the fly line with the tube or needle knot. Since the tube not is not as functional, use the needle knot.

Leader to Fly Line

3. NEEDLE KNOT (LEADER TO FLY LINE)

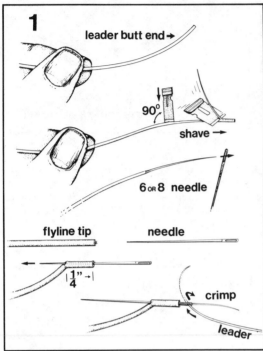

leader butt end →

90°

shave →

6 or 8 needle

flyline tip   needle

|← 1" →|
    4

crimp

leader

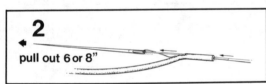

2

pull out 6 or 8"

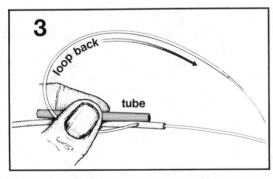

3

loop back

tube

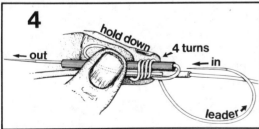

4

hold down   4 turns

← out   → in

leader ↗

1A. *Begin by removing the leader from its package and straightening out about twelve to eighteen inches of the butt or thick end. You can straighten the butt by stroking it with your hand until you feel it warm up. Then stretch it tight and hold it in that position until it cools (about five to ten seconds).*

1B. *Now, using a very sharp razor blade, catch the leader two inches from butt end and shave down the end of the leader's butt so that it will pass through the eye of a size 6, 7, or 8 darning needle. Hold the leader butt with your thumb and index fingers so that four to six inches extend out away from you. The best method to "shave" the leader is as follows: Hold the razor blade (a single edge is safest) between the thumb and index fingers of your other hand, which should be your writing hand. About 1½ to two inches from the butt end, at a 90° angle, touch the razor to the leader and at 10° to 15° degrees shave smoothly and slowly forward while pulling the butt backward. You are trying to slice a small section of the leader away evenly. Make a one-third rotation of the butt and repeat this shaving process until the end will fit through the needle's eye.*

1C. *Next, slightly dull the point of a size 6, 7, and 8 darning needle with a nail file, sharpening stone, or other such tool. Try to select a needle that has an eye the same diameter as its shaft so that it will easily pass up through and out the side of the fly-line tip.*

1D. *Stick the needle point into the end of the fly-line tip, centering it on the line's braided core. Push the point about one-eighth or one-quarter inch up the fly-line tip and out the fly-line's side, as shown in the diagram. With fingers or pliers pull all but the needle's eye through the fly-line tip end. Push one-half to one inch of the trimmed butt into the exposed needle's eye, and crimp so it won't slide out before the next step.*

2. *Now, with your fingers or, better, a pair of small pliers, pull the needle's eye up through the fly line and out the side. Remove the leader butt from the needle and then pull about six to eight inches of the untrimmed butt through the fly-line tip and out the side.*

From here on, the completion of the needle knot parallels the steps used for the tube knot with which you joined the line and backing. Use the same holding and wrapping procedures.

3. *Hold fly-line tip in left index finger and thumb. Place the two-inch-long tube parallel and next to fly-line's tip. Loop leader butt between holding fingers back toward fly-line tip and tube end.*

4. *Wrap the leader butt up, over, and around the fly-line tip and tube four full turns, advancing toward the fly-line tip and right end of tube. Be sure to hold each wrap firmly with thumb and index and middle fingers. Try to position consecutive wraps close together. (If you relax your grip, the stiff nylon leader butt will uncoil in an instant and come off the line and tube.) Now pass the leader butt end through the tube.*

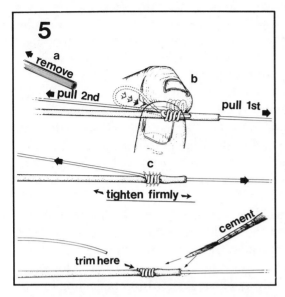

5A. *Remove the tube to the left from your fingers and the fly-line tip.*

5B. *After the tube is removed (while you retain a firm grip on the line and the leader wraps), pull first on the leader section that comes off the fly-line tip. Second, pull on the butt end of the leader. Pull just firmly enough to snug wraps against fly-line. Now carefully release your hold, slide the wraps down toward the tip of the fly-line to the point just over where the leader comes out of the fly-line side.*

5C. *Tighten the wraps at this point by first pulling on the leader coming out of the fly-line tip and then on the tag end of the leader butt behind the knot. You will need a small pair of pliers to tighten down the nylon wraps if the butt end of the leader is especially stiff and thick. Be sure, however, not to over-tighten, for the knot will pinch or cut into the vinyl coating of the fly-line tip. Trim excess leader end away at knot. For best results coat the needle knot with head cement or clear fingernail polish and allow it to dry.*

For fly-line tips that are not hollow, use tube knot.

After you finish tying the fly-line-tip-to-leader knot, reel on the leader except for about 24 inches of leader tip, which you will need for tying the leader-tip-to-tippet knot.

Some leaders come with the appropriate size of leader tip for fly-fishing; however, you may want to add a tippet while fishing because the tip has been broken off or because you want a longer or lighter tippet. You can use the *surgeon's knot* for tying the tippet to the leader tip.

Leader to Tippet

SURGEON'S KNOT

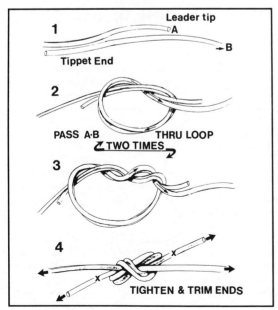

1. *Begin by cutting a length of monofilament of the appropriate size from the leader spool—make it about eight to twelve inches longer than you want your finished tippet, to allow for length loss when tying. Take an eighteen- to twenty-four-inch section of the leader-tippet material, and place one end parallel to the leader's tip (so that A and B sections are four to five inches apart).*

2. *Grasp leader and tippet ends with thumb and index fingers. With your other hand, form a common open loop of the two with its opening under or below the parallel of the two.*

3. *Now pass sections A and B completely through the open loop twice.*

4. *Wet the loop with your lips and pull the paired strands of tip and tippet briskly to tighten the knot. Wetting allows the line to tighten smoothly without damage. Trim the tag end close to the knot.*

SURGEON'S LOOP

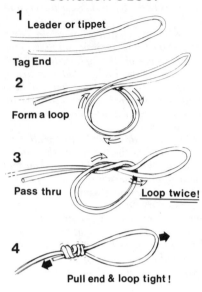

1 Leader or tippet

Tag End

2 Form a loop

3 Pass thru — Loop twice!

4 Pull end & loop tight !

Fly to Leader

This surgeon's knot is generally recommended over the more traditional blood knot because it is simpler and faster to tie. Further, it is smaller than the blood knot and can be used with more sizes and types of monofilament much better than the blood knot.

You can modify the surgeon's knot to form the **surgeon's loop** as shown in the accompanying illustration. By making a loop at the end of the leader and one at the end of the tippet, you can join the two by means of interlocking loops. Loop-to-loop connections are useful for quick changes to new or different size tippets.

If the tackle is not to be used immediately for fishing, reel the leader onto the spool, leaving about six inches of leader free. Place this through one of the reel-spool holes or tape it to the spool side. This tactic prevents the end of the leader from becoming lost in the line on the reel or getting caught in the reel spool.

There are at least a dozen practical knots for tying the fly to the leader tippet. We recommend three. The Duncan loop is the most practical. The improved turle and improved clinch knots are two others that work well.

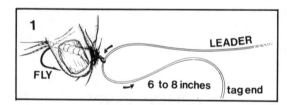

1 FLY — LEADER — 6 to 8 inches — tag end

2 hold here — 2" tag — form — loop — 1½"

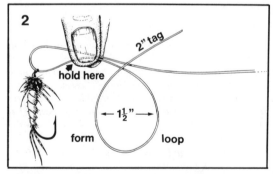

3 5 turns of tag →

5.

THE DUNCAN LOOP

1. Hold fly in left-hand thumb and index fingers with hook down and hook eye forward and exposed. Pass tag end of leader (tippet) down through top side of hook's eye a length of six or eight inches.

2. Move your left-hand finger grip forward onto the leader strands just ahead of the hook's eye. Study diagram. With your right-hand fingers form a 1½-inch-diameter loop with the six to eight inches of tag end just ahead of your left-hand hold on the leader. Loop's tag end should now be pointing away from fly and about two inches long.

3. With left-hand thumb and index finger grasp the leader and loop together. Place middle fingers of both hands in loop to keep it open and secure. With right-hand thumb and index fingers pass the leader's tag end over, around, and through leader and loop five times.

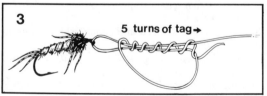

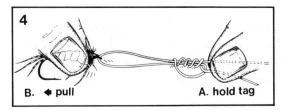

4

B. ← pull   A. hold tag

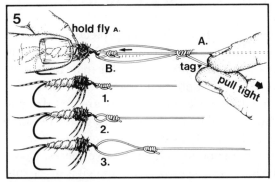

5

hold fly A.

A.

B.

tag

pull tight

1.

2.

3.

4A. With right thumb and index fingers firmly hold tag end and leader and remove middle fingers from loop.

4B. Hold fly with left hand and pull it left to begin reducing loop and drawing knot tight. Wet wraps with mouth to lubricate them for easier and better tightening. Do not pull on tag end at this point or an excess amount of leader waste will occur.

5A. To pull knot down, tighten and pull hard on tag end. Degree of tightening determines how knot slips along leader—the tighter the knot the less slippage the loop will have. Once the tag end is tightened, clip away its excess length.

5B. Adjust loop's size by holding leader in right hand. With the left hand grasp the knot and slide it closer or further away from the fly. If a more or less stationary or fixed loop size is desired, pull very hard on tag end once desired loop size is formed. If loop has one or more twists in it, simply slide the knot tight against the fly's eye before final tag-tightening is done. This removes the twists and you may open again to desired size.

NOTE: *Once a fish is hooked or fly is hooked on an object, the line and rod pressures usually close the loop. Simply grasp the knot and slide it away from hook eye to desired loop size. Very heavy leaders (12-pound test and over) only require three or four turns. Very light leaders (1 to 2-pound test) may require six or seven turns for best knot performance.*

KNOT OPTIONS:

A. *Loop clinched down snug against hook's eye; leader holds fly tightly to it.*

B. *Small open tight loop gives fly freedom to move independently of leader.*

C. *Large loose loop acts as slip/shock absorber to prevent breaking of leader during hard strikes.*

Another good knot for tying the fly to the tippet is the *improved clinch knot*. This is a standard fisherman's knot, and it is simple to tie. It does have some tightening and slipping disadvantages. Also, the tight knot on the hook eye inhibits movement and tends to change the balance of the fly. The improved clinch knot balances or works best on ring-eye hooks. When used with turned-down eye or turned-up eye hooks, this knot may cause unbalance and the fly to float or swim poorly when you are fishing it.

A third knot for tying the fly to the tippet is the *improved turle knot*. This knot should be used only with turned-up or turned-down eye hooks. It provides a straight pull on fly, hook, and leader. It does not attach to the hook eye, but rather it holds to the fly's head. This arrangement reduces wear on the nylon leader by eliminating contact with the hook eye during casting and fishing, and it does not affect the fly's balance. But like the improved clinch knot, the improved turle knot does inhibit the natural action of the fly.

All knots that are tied with nylon monofilament should be moistened before they are drawn tight. And

IMPROVED CLINCH KNOT

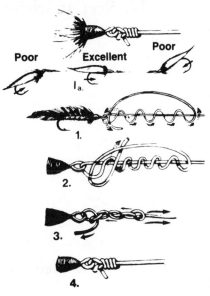

Poor   Excellent   Poor

I a.

1.

2.

3.

4.

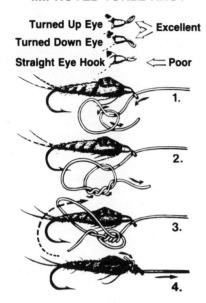

IMPROVED TURLE KNOT

Turned Up Eye — Excellent

Turned Down Eye

Straight Eye Hook — Poor

1.

2.

3.

4.

Fly-Rod Assembly

Fly-Reel Attachment

Leader straightening

when drawing them tight, you should pull them slowly. After this initial tightening, test the knot with a mild series of irregular pulls. Check your knots and leader regularly during use.

Assembling Fly Tackle for Use

After removing the fly rod from its protective tube and its cloth cover, fit the tip and butt sections together as directed by the manufacturer. Insert the male ferrule into the female ferrule until resistance is felt. Align the guides on the different sections so they are in a straight line; you can adjust the alignment with a gentle twisting motion. Once the guides are aligned, apply a bit more pressure to the ferrule to tighten the two pieces. Don't worry if the male ferrule seems a bit long; it is made this way to compensate for wear.

If the ferrules fit together loosely, take the rod apart and apply a film of beeswax on the male ferrule; this will usually tighten up the fit without damage. Also, if the ferrules feel gritty when you're putting them together, take them apart and clean them with soap and water. A cotton swab is excellent for cleaning inside the female ferrule.

Once the rod sections are together, attach the reel as previously described. Next, find the leader tip on the reel. Holding the rod handle, pull out the entire length of leader and 1½ times the rod length of fly line. Now place the reel and handle end of the rod on a clean, flat, non-abrasive surface (or have a companion hold it). Hold the rod near the ferrule, and grasp the fly line two or three feet from the leader. Thread the doubled-over line through the guides toward the tip, taking care not to wrap the line around the rod between guides. Pull the loose line and leader through the guides as you advance toward the tip. When you have passed two feet of the fly line through the tip-top, release it and give the rod a couple of quick casting motions. The loose line between reel and tip will quickly clear the rod tip.

The leader and fly line will have developed a coil set from being stored on the reel spool. This set must be straightened out for best performance. To do this, have someone hold the fly line or attach it to a door handle or another firm structure so that you can straighten the leader. Stroke the leader with your hand until you feel it warm up. Hold the leader straight and tight for a few seconds as it cools to reset the leader in a straight condition. Repeat until most of the coils or kinks are removed.

Fly line straightening

Next, over a clean surface pull thirty to fifty feet of fly line off the reel. Have someone hold one end or else attach it to a firm structure. Then pull the fly line tight until you feel it stretch just a bit. Hold it stretched for several seconds, release tension, and see if the line has straightened. If it has not, repeat this procedure or stretch and gently stroke the line surface. A fly line is particularly difficult to straighten when it is cold (below 45 °F). When the air or water temperature is near or below freezing, the fly-line finish becomes hard. Under such conditions, the line is easily cracked during stretching or fishing. To prevent cracking damage, avoid excessive stretching.

Fly to Leader

Now you are ready to tie on the fly, using one of the knots previously recommended. If you are just going to practice casting, you can tie on a practice fly. The practice fly should have no point and no barb. Such a fly will prevent hooking and hangups.

When two or more anglers are present, one person can hold the rod while you thread the line through the guides, which ensures that the fly reel remains clean.

When you assemble your fly tackle for use, you should take care to place the empty cloth sack back into the fly-rod tube. Put the lid back on the tube and you will make certain that the cloth sack does not get wet or dirty or lost.

Dissassembling Fly Tackle

Proper disassembly of fly tackle is also important. It helps you prevent damage and ensures that the tackle will be ready the next time you want to use it.

When you are about to end a fishing session, reel in your line and make a few short, rapid false-casts to dry off the fly before removing it. Cut the fly off the tippet and place it in a hatband, on your fishing vest's fly patch, or in a well-ventilated fly box so it will dry completely.

Drying and Cleaning Fly Line

To clean and dry the fly line, first lay it over the water or over a grit-free surface. With a clean cloth or paper towel in your rod hand, reel the fly line onto the reel spool while squeezing it with the towel. This removes most of the water and the dirty film a line acquires during fishing. Always make sure when you reel the fly line onto the reel that it spools onto the reel firmly and evenly. Guide it with your rod hand, using moderate tension. Too loose or uneven spooling may cause a difficult tangle. If the fly line is wound on too tight, however, it may kink or set in small loops or curls.

Leader-reel storage

As you wind the leader onto the fly reel, leave out about four to six inches of the tippet. This makes the fine tippet end much easier to find next time, and it also prevents the end from accidentally passing under the leader or line coils on the reel. If the leader slips under a coil of line on the reel, it is possible that a half-hitch will result causing a tangle and/or loss of a large fish. Take the end of the leader and pass it out on one of the reel-spool ventilation holes and back in another to keep it in place and prevent its getting lost in the spool.

Fly-Reel Storage

Now remove the reel from the reel seat, wipe it clean and dry it with a towel. Place the reel in a well-ventilated bag or case to allow the damp fly line and backing and the internal parts of the reel to dry.

Disassembling Fly Rod

Now disassemble the rod. If the ferrules seem stuck, have a companion help you separate them—both of you should hold on to a different section of the rod and then pull slowly. Wipe the fly rod clean and dry with a towel. Replace it in the cloth rod bag and protective case. Be sure not to get the rod case of the rod bag wet. When storing the rod tube with the cloth sack and fly rod inside, you can leave the lid of the tube off to make sure that the rod bag, the inside of the rod tube, and the fly rod dry. It is essential that the rod and cloth bag be dry.

Store your tackle in a dark, cool, dry area. Proper storage prevents damage and premature aging.

Always disassemble sections of your fly rod when storing it in a boat, car, or cabin or when carrying it through dense foliage. Car doors, house doors, feet, and tree limbs are famous for their ability to break fly rods. Many more fly rods are broken as a result of carelessness than by fish and fishing.

2

How To Fly-Cast

Learning to fly-cast is easiest when you understand the basic dynamics. To the casual observer or the inexperienced fly-caster, casting appears to be a back-and-forth waving of a rod to cast the fly and the fly line. That is not correct. Proper fly-casting requires specifically coordinated arm, wrist, hand, and rod movement to accomplish line pickup, backcast, forward cast, and presentation of the fly.

Unlike casting methods that use the lure's weight to cast, fly-casting uses the line's weight to cast. The fly line pulls an almost weightless fly along with it. There are two complete strokes in fly-casting; the backcast and the forward cast. The fly follows the fly line as the line straightens in either direction.

Loop control is the key to fly-casting. As the rod is cast backward or forward, the fly line follows each stroke forming an unrolling loop. The shape and

Basic Loop Shapes of Backcast and Forecast

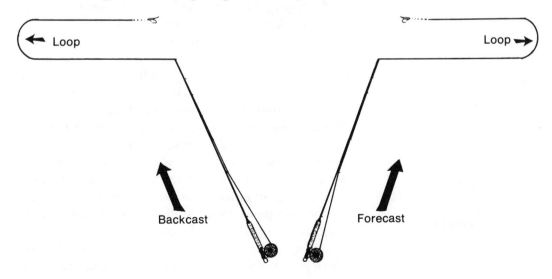

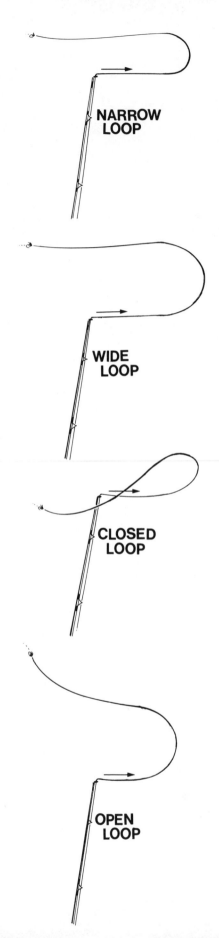

NARROW LOOP

WIDE LOOP

CLOSED LOOP

OPEN LOOP

direction of the loop as it unrolls largely determines the success of the cast. A good fly caster knows how to control this loop. There are four general loop types: a narrow loop, a wide loop, a closed (or tailing) loop, and an open loop.

The loop is formed by the arc that the rod tip makes as power is applied from your arm and wrist movements. All arm and wrist movement should be back and forth in the same plane. Any lateral movement of the tip during the power stroke will influence the loop's shape and the direction of line movement. Generally speaking, the smaller the arc, the narrower the loop will be; the larger the arc, the wider the loop will be.

The narrow loop is more efficient in turning over the line and leader and presenting the fly. The wide loop creates more air resistance and is far less efficient in casting and presentation. A closed loop creates the same air resistance problems as well as tangling and poor presentation.

The simplest way to relate loop control to casting-stroke control is to use what is known as the clock system. Visualize yourself standing with a large clock face beside you. The nine o'clock position is forward (the direction you are facing), twelve o'clock directly above your head, three o'clock behind you, and six o'clock at your feet.

The narrow loop you desire is accomplished by beginning the backcast with the rod at eleven o'clock and stopping it at one o'clock. Do not allow the rod tip to move farther than the two o'clock position as the fly-line loop unrolls behind you. Watch the back loop unroll, and just as it nears the end, begin to pull the rod forward slowly. Do not wait for a tug. When your rod tip reaches the one o'clock position, slowly begin to apply power to the forward casting stroke. Come forward smoothly, making sure not to shock the rod. Gradually increase the rod speed (or power) until you reach the eleven o'clock position. Now stop the forward stroke and keep the rod tip high until the loop unrolls in front of you. The stop or pause on backward or forward power strokes allows the fly-line loop to form and progress past the rod tip.

If you use these directions in short casting strokes, the loop size will be ideal. If you use a longer arc, that

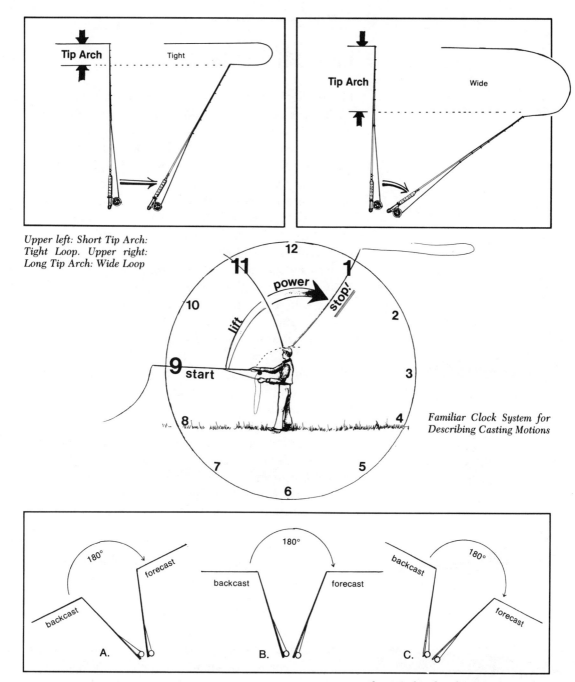

Upper left: Short Tip Arch: Tight Loop. Upper right: Long Tip Arch: Wide Loop

Familiar Clock System for Describing Casting Motions

The 180° of Back and Forecasting Strokes, at Various Cast Angles

is, a backward stroke from nine to three o'clock and forward stroke from three to nine o'clock—the loop will be wider. A tailing loop is caused by starting the forward stroke too soon or applying full power too soon. For ideal loop control, you should make your backcast and forward cast directly in line with each other.

Basic Fly-Casting Procedure

Before beginning this section on fly-casting procedure, be sure that you understand the previous section on fly-casting dynamics. It is best to begin your initial fly-casting practice under the instruction of a qualified fly-casting instructor—preferably not a spouse or fly-fishing friend. A spouse or friend may cause unnecessary emotional pressure. If friends want to help you, make sure that first they read and understand this section on fly-casting theory and method so they will not confuse you. It is better for you to understand this text and go it alone than to accept the help of an unqualified instructor.

Begin by choosing a water area that has an uncongested, calm, non-flowing surface—such as a pond, lake, or swimming pool. The area should also have an unrestricted space of at least 40 feet behind you and 20 feet to either side. Make sure there are no limbs, wires, or other obstructions above you. If such an area is not available, you may practice on a lawn or a gymnasium floor. If you are casting over the ground, and the ground is muddy, rough, or oily, spread out a groundcloth or canvas. This will protect your fly line from damage and becoming dirty. In any instance, try to practice when there is little or no wind. If you cannot escape the wind, try to position yourself so that it blows from your left side if you cast with your right arm, and vice versa.

It is very important when practicing fly-casting to use a fly or practice fly of an appropriate type and size. Without a fly, the tackle does not cast correctly, and it will mislead your learning responses. To avoid accidents, you can use a fly whose point and barb have been removed. Simply cut the hook at the bend. If you want, you can tie about two inches of colorful yarn to the leader tip. Now straighten your leader and about 40 feet of the fly line.

Five Types of Hookless Practice Flies

Dry Fly

Streamer

Wet Fly

Bug

Saltwater Fly

Simple Way to Make a Hookless Fly

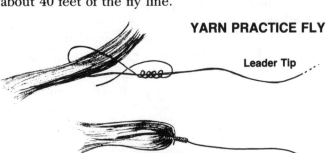

YARN PRACTICE FLY

Leader Tip

While holding the rod handle in your casting hand (your master hand or writing hand), strip about 30 feet of fly line off the reel with the other hand. Let this line fall to the ground at your feet. Grasp the fly and leader and pull about 20 feet of fly line out through the tip-top. This is the initial amount of fly line you will need to start casting.

Facing the direction in which you intend to cast, place your feet about 1½ feet apart and have your casting-arm foot a bit behind the other. If you are casting over water, stand about three or four feet from the edge in a clear, clean area so that excess line does not tangle or become dirty. By positioning your feet as recommended, you will be standing slightly sideways of the direction in which you intend to cast. This stance is necessary to allow you to watch your forward cast and backcast unroll. You cannot learn to fly-cast well if you do not observe both your forward and backward casts.

Hold the fly rod, reel, and line as shown in the accompanying illustration. Make sure that your thumb is on top of the rod handle and that you have positioned your grip on the handle comfortably. Try to avoid placing your index finger on the top of the handle, for this position will not give you the stability you need. Hold the fly line between the reel and the first stripping guide with your other hand to maintain line control.

Preparing to Practice Casting

Proper Method of Holding Fly Rod and Fly Line for Ideal Control While Fly Casting

A. Hand hold on fly rod

B. Hand hold on fly line

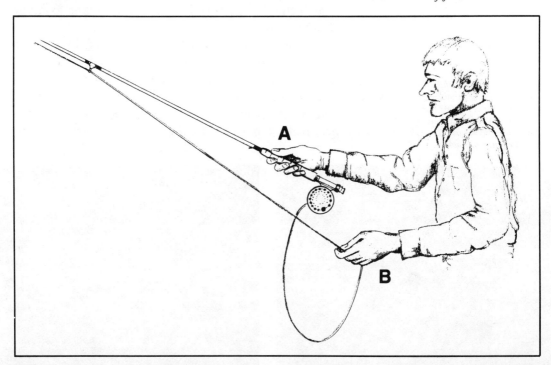

Top left: *Thumb grip. For best casting grip, place thumb on top of handle and forward of reel. This grip gives a caster maximum control and power.* Top right: *Index finger on top and forward may seem more comfortable and accurate, but it limits strength, control, and stability between rod and caster's hand and arm. This grip is satisfactory for light rods and short distances but it will tire your hand if you use it for any length of time.* Lower left: *The split grip limits control and strength, causing many faults to develop. Hand tires quickly.*

Before starting to cast, take a couple of slow, deep breaths and relax. Lift the fly rod and fly line with a smooth motion, using your wrist, arm, and shoulder in an up and back direction to place the rod and line into the right "clock" position. You should keep the rod in a vertical or slightly to the side angle, as shown in clock-position illustration. Stop at two o'clock. Watch the fly line travel back until it begins to fall or straighten out.

Just as it does, begin the forward cast by moving your arm and fly rod forward with a gradual acceleration—not full speed immediately. When the arm and rod move just past the forward point of your shoulder and chest, bring your wrist crisply forward from the one o'clock position to the eleven o'clock position.

Lower left: *Begin pickup for cast by pointing rod tip low (about eight o'clock) and forward.* Lower right: *Raise rod tip horizontally up to lift fly line off water before beginning back cast. Do not pass eleven o'clock point on pickup.*

Now stop the rod's forward progress. Watch the fly line move forward, unrolling and straightening itself. At this stage, make sure that you are always holding on to the fly line on both the pickup/backcast and the forward cast with your line hand.

Just as the fly line begins to drop or is about to unroll completely, begin to pull arm and rod back to start a second backcast. Repeat the backcast procedure, watching the fly line over your shoulder as you do so. The casting strokes are similar to tossing stones or driving a small nail with a hammer. Repeat the forward and backcasting strokes several times, trying to get the fly line to form a narrow, smooth loop that stays aloft at rod-tip height. If the line does not unroll before it begins to drop, use more power (or speed) on the eleven o'clock to one o'clock stroke and on the one o'clock to eleven o'clock stroke.

Watch your line and the rod-tip position constantly and you will be able to correct most of your initial mistakes. Too much rod-tip arc and not enough power are the main problems of inexperienced fly casters. Watching your back and forward casts will enable you to detect and correct these problems.

Keep your casting arm in a comfortable position as you practice. The fly rod's path should allow you to feel most relaxed during the forward and backward strokes.

Fly-casting practice should include presenting the

When the fly line comes to its highest lift point off the water in front of you, begin the backcast stroke immediately with a smooth accelerating power stroke between eleven and one o'clock. Watch rod tip and fly line.

Lower left: *As rod tip stops between one and two o'clock, backcast loop forms (note its path and shape) and travels back.* Lower right: *Just as the line tip and leader begin to unroll, start forward cast by gradual forward acceleration from two to one o'clock. This move straightens the fly line and loads fly rod for forward cast.*

fly, leader, and line to the fishing area or target. Presentation begins with the direction of the forward cast. This determines where the line, leader, and fly will go. As you complete the forward power stroke, stopping the rod tip at eleven o'clock, let the loop unroll. Do not immediately follow through by continuing the motion downward with the fly rod. Let the fly line unroll; only when it begins to decelerate and fall should you follow it down with rod tip to about eight o'clock. This tactic allows the loop to unroll completely out to the leader and fly. If you lower your rod tip too quickly, you will ruin the presentation by driving the loop to the water before it unrolls.

If the leader and fly do not unroll and straighten out before they land, falling near or behind the fly-line tip, you need to apply more power (create greater line speed). Also, make sure your loop is narrow. If the fly line, leader, and fly seem to jerk or recoil back toward you, you are probably using too much power or not following through by lowering the rod tip as the fly line unrolls and falls.

As you begin practicing, it is very important to use only twenty to thirty feet of fly line. Don't be tempted to use more. As soon as you exceed this length, you run the hazard of using more fly line than you can easily handle. You will surely encounter problems that will hinder your timing, loop control, and presentation.

As the fly lands on the water, it is important to have

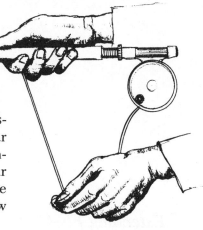

full line control immediately. An accompanying illustration shows how to place the fly line under your casting-hand index finger. This tactic gives you a constant antireverse and slack-line control. You use your line hand to retrieve the fly; you need only relax the tension on the line with your rod-hand finger to allow stripping line in.

It is a good idea at this stage to practice your fly presentation so that you learn all of the basic techniques together. This will prove to be less monotonous than simply practicing your casting. You will also be practicing casting, presentation, and fishing in the same sequence in which they occur during actual fishing.

You can control the fly's position and action by using the fly-rod length and the angle at which you hold it. The rod tip can be used to give the fly action—as you might give action to a puppet on a string. You should also practice moving and retrieving the fly by making pulls of various lengths and speeds on the fly line through the index finger of your rod hand. You can practice hooking a fish by practicing a

Two-Point Positive Method of Rod and Line Control for Fly Fishing, Retrieving and Hooking

Upper left: *Proper rod and fly-line grip for pickup, casting, and line shooting.* Upper right: *Proper two-hand grip for controling line in fishing, fly retrieving, and line shooting.* Lower left: *Proper grip for retrieving slack line onto fly reel. The slack line between fly reel and rod hand is held with rod hand's small finger to control fly line's tension and position of reel spool. In fighting fish or simply recovering excess fly line, this prevents line from being spooled in tangles, too loose, or unevenly.* Lower Right: *Proper rod and reel grips to use in retrieving or giving out fly line that is under tension from a fighting fish.*

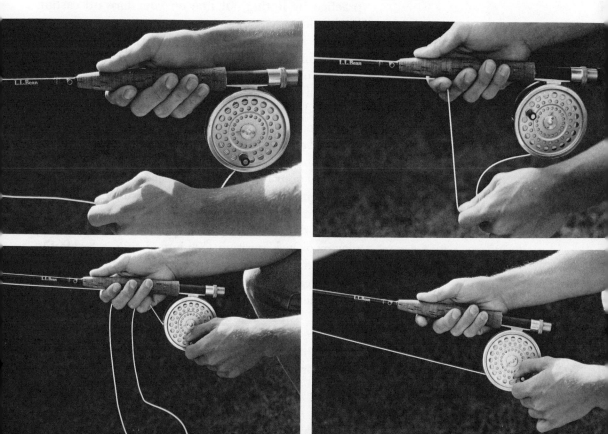

crisp upward or sideways movement of the rod tip and/or a crisp, foot-long pull on the fly line with your line hand through your relaxed rod-hand index finger.

Practice all these casting procedures repeatedly, remembering to stay relaxed and stopping to rest when you get confused or a little arm weary. Watch your casting loops, especially the backcast loop! It is the key to fast learning.

Extending Fly-Cast Distance

If you have retrieved a few feet of fly line when practicing fishing and you wish to cast it out or add length to the line you are casting, here is how to do it. On your backward or forward power stroke—eleven o'clock to one o'clock or one o'clock to eleven o'clock—increase the power of your stroke over what is needed to cast the length of fly line you have already out. Just after *but not during* the power stroke, release your grip on the fly line enough to allow the moving fly line to pull out extra line. Remember: release your grip after the power stroke has been completed. It is the weight of the fly line moving forward or backward that pulls the extra slack line from your hand. If you wish to put out more than several feet of fly line, it may be necessary to let out slack on two or more casting strokes. But you should practice by letting out line on your forward casting stroke alone.

Fly-line Pickup Practice

If you are practicing over water, you should—after completing several practice cycles—practice picking the line off the water correctly. Proper fly line pickup is critical to proper casting technique.

A good pickup begins with your fly rod in the eight o'clock position—or the rod's tip a few inches above the water's surface. Release the rod finger's hold on the fly line and at the same time make a pull on the fly line with your line hand. This maneuver removes any slack from the fly line on the water and begins to load the fly rod's tip. Raise the fly rod immediately with a smooth, deliberate—but not quick—motion up to the eleven o'clock position. Your objective is to lift the extended fly line off or away from the water's surface-tension grip. From the eleven o'clock position, begin to accelerate the rod backward to the one o'clock position, using your arm and shoulder for power. This sequence tightens the line, lifts it off the water, and puts it into the proper backcast angle.

This procedure is emphasized here to forestall pos-

The Basic Roll Cast

Step 1: (Top) *Begin roll cast with 20 to 30 feet of fly line extended. Lower the rod tip to eight-o'clock position, and tighten the fly line between the rod's tip and the fly by pulling on the fly line with line hand.*

Step 2: (Mid left) *In a smooth slow motion, lift rod up and back, slightly to your side and into the one-o'clock casting position. Give fly line time enough to pull into a wide arc at your right on water up to rod's tip. Without stopping or hesitating, proceed immediately to Step 3.*

Step 3: (Mid right) *With an accelerating power stroke, go from one o'clock to eleven o'clock, just as you would in a regular tight-loop forward cast, but do it all a bit more slowly.*

Step 4: (Lower left) *Allow the loop to form forward and roll forward by stopping the rod's forward stroke by at least ten o'clock. Be careful not to overdrive the rod too low, which prevents loop and roll from forming properly.*

Step 5: (Lower right) *As loop rolls forward to target, lower rod slowly for proper presentation.*

Note: *Practice roll casting on water only. On dry or slick surfaces, the slipping line will not load the rod properly, as it does when held by the water's surface tension.*

sible bad habits. After a few water or land pickups, you will otherwise tend to start your backcast power stroke while the fly line and rod tip are too low— resulting in a very poor initial backcast, which destroys your overall casting success.

Types of Fly Casts

All fly-casting revolves around the basic backward and forward casting strokes and the control of loop size, direction, and speed. Your eyes, legs, shoulder, arm, wrist, and hand should all combine to energize and control the rod to cast the fly line, its leader, and the fly to the target area.

False-casting means fly-casting backward and forward without actually presenting the fly to the target area. It is useful when you wish to gain distance by working out more line, when you aim the fly over a certain target, or when you want to remove water from a dry fly or a hair bug. False-casting is also useful when practicing your loop control and fly-casting technique. When you are fishing, however, too much false-casting can cause fatigue or poor timing. If you use the false cast sparingly, it will serve you well.

Roll-casting is a modification of the standard casting technique. In a roll cast, the fly line *is not lifted* from the water for the backcast but is simply pulled back along the water and then cast forward. The usual forward casting stroke is made, and the line rolls out in front of you. Roll-casting is used to best advantage when backcasting room is unavailable or when strong winds behind you make backcasting impractical. The roll cast is also useful when lifting up a sinking fly line before making a standard pickup into the backcast.

A *curve cast* bends to the right or left of you and is a variation of the standard forward casting stroke. A portion of the line tip, leader, and the fly curves to the right or left from the general direction of the power casting stroke. Curve casts are useful when presenting the fly around surface objects or when preventing the leader and fly line from being seen by a fish as the fly passes over the fish.

A *slack-line* or *serpent cast* is another variation on the standard forward cast, this one causing the line to fall on the water in a series of curves or Ss. Such a cast allows the fly to float without dragging and is especially useful when casting across current or directly downstream.

Reach casting allows the fly, leader, and line to be presented to a target area at an extreme right-hand or left-hand angle from the caster. It is especially useful when presenting a fly across a stream that has several current speeds. Reach casting prevents the fly from dragging downstream faster than the water on which it lands.

Shooting line is similar in purpose to working out line. It is accomplished in either the backward or forward cast by using considerably more power than is needed to cast the line already extended. In either the backward or forward cast, slack line is fed out just as the moving loop reaches its end, thus pulling or shooting the extra slack out with it. Generally, shooting line out reduces the number of false casts needed and aids casting distance.

Hauling is a technique of increasing line speed or overall fly-casting efficiency by using the power of both the rod arm and the free hand arm. To accomplish a haul: the caster, just as the power stroke is applied with the fly rod, simultaneously pulls down on the taut fly line below the first stripper guide. This pull—or haul—increases the line's forward or backward speed. Double-hauling involves hauling on both the forward and backward strokes. Hauling should not be attempted until you have mastered loop control. Only then does it become a useful method for better line pickup and for making long, powerful casts. If you try hauling before you have mastered loop control, it will have an adverse effect on your overall casting ability.

Mending line is a technique of repositioning the fly line and leader on moving water. It is accomplished by using various rod-lifting and roll-casting movements. When you are fishing streams, mending line is about as important as casting.

Common Fly-Casting Problems and Solutions

Proper fly-casting technique takes patience and practice to acquire. You will encounter many problems along the way to achieving proficiency. Here are some of the most common problems that beginners encounter. Each is followed by its solution.

Problem: Fly line, leader, and fly will not go out the desired distance (20 to 60 feet). This is usually the beginner's first problem, and it usually is caused by inefficient casting technique or improperly balanced tackle or both.

Solution: Make sure the rod and fly-line sizes are properly matched. Too light a line for a rod will cause casting problems of this nature. Work on tighter loop control and better timing of power application on both the forward and backward casting strokes.

Problem: Fly hits the water behind the caster.

Solution: This problem usually results from inefficiency in the backcast. Check to see that you are lifting the fly line off the water before your rod tip reaches the twelve o'clock position. Also check how far behind you the rod tip is going. Practice a smooth fly-line pickup at the beginning of the backcast, and stop the power stroke at the one o'clock position. Look back to see if your backcast has enough power to unroll before it begins to fall behind you.

Problem: Leader and fly line splash down too hard or before they completely unroll and straighten out.

Solution: This problem usually indicates that you are overpowering your forward stroke, thus overdriving the line and leader to the water before the loop unrolls. Stop the power stroke higher and slow the rod's follow-through to the nine o'clock position. Concentrate on letting the line and leader straighten out above the water.

Problem: Fly, leader, and line strike the rod.

Solution: If the line or leader strikes the rod on the forward or backward cast, you need more power or a smoother power stroke. When lifting line from the water, lift the fly line by raising the rod butt and your arm before you begin to backcast. Now simply apply more power to the power stroke when casting.

Problem: Tailing loop.

Solution: This problem usually results when a fly caster begins a power stroke before either the backcast or forward loop unrolls. With a better caster, the problem is most commonly a result of applying the power to the rod too quickly rather than allowing the power to increase smoothly through the stroke. Watch your loops unroll, and start the power stroke slowly just as the line tip and leader are unrolling. Or practice a more gradual power stroke with the fly rod. Beginning a stroke too fast will shock the rod's tip and cause it to recoil, which may form a tailing loop.

Problem: Leader wind knots or fly-line tangles occur while casting.

Solution: This problem has the same causes as tailing loops and can be corrected in the same manner.

Problem: Too wide a loop.

Solution: This problem results from a power stroke arc that is too wide. The loop size will be proportional to the stroke size. Practice the clock method of power stroke arc between the eleven o'clock and one o'clock positions.

Problem: Open loop.

Solution: This problem is caused by too wide an arc when casting—or starting the casting stroke too late. It may be solved in the same manner as the problem of casting too wide a loop.

Problem: Fly snaps off on backcast or makes a cracking noise on backcast.

Solution: This happens when you start the forward cast too soon, before the line has unrolled and straightened behind you. This problem is very similar to the tailing loop problem and can be corrected in the same manner. Get into the habit of watching your backcast. You will notice that the fly-snapping problem and line-cracking problem does not occur on the forward loop, because you watch it unroll before beginning the next stroke.

Problem: Fly and leader twist and tangle. This happens when you use a fly that spins as it is cast.

Solution: Use a fly that is designed better, or use a larger-diameter, stiffer tippet. If you can't do either, make slower casts and reduce or eliminate false-casting.

Lower left: This back cast loop is much too wide. If the rod tip goes below two o'clock during power stroke, a slow and inefficient wide loop is the result. A poor back cast loop significantly hampers forward cast efficiency. Note rod angle is at three o'clock. If you will watch your backcast, you can easily correct this fault.

Lower right: *The loop on this forward cast is too wide. If rod tip goes past eleven o'clock on power stroke (as shown here), the result is an inefficient loop that limits casting distance, hampers fly turnover, and reduces accuracy. Note that rod tip is at nine o'clock.*

Wind Casting

Excessive wind from any direction causes casting problems. In most instances, you can use the wind to advantage.

Problem: When the wind is in your face, it blows the fly and line back at you when you cast forward.

Solution: To avoid this, reduce the height and angle of your forward cast and increase the power of the casting stroke. Increase the height and angle of the backcast. This tactic puts the forward line under most of the wind's force to assist the backcast.

Problem: When the wind is at your back, it blows the fly line down, causing it to strike your back or the fly rod on a forward stroke.

Solution: To solve this problem, make a lower-angle, tight-looped, powerful backcast to reduce wind drag on the line and to keep the line out of the wind's full force. On the forward cast make a higher-angle power stroke to let the wind strength lift and turn over the line, leader, and fly.

Problem: When the wind is from your casting-arm side, it blows the line across your body and head, often tangling up or hooking you.

Solution: To correct this, keep the rod and arm high and angled over you to the other side or use a back-hand casting technique. You can also use the opposite arm for casting. These adaptations place the line on the downwind side of you and prevent it from striking you.

Problem: When the wind blows from your free-arm side, the line is blown low and to the side, causing a presentation problem or the possibility of hooking someone on that side of you.

Solution: To solve this problem, use a sidearm cast to reduce the fly-line height, which avoids the wind's full force. The fly line is blown out farther to that side, so you only need to compensate for extra wind lead.

The wind's force against any cast is best countered by a very tight-looped, low, and powerful cast. If you regularly fly-fish in very windy areas, you should also consider using heavier line weights to gain more casting power against the wind. It is very hard to make long and accurate casts against the wind. But if you follow these suggestions, there is no reason why you cannot enjoy fly-casting in normal winds.

3

Fly-Fishing Tactics

Fishing the fly is as important as casting the fly. Unless you intend to fly-cast only in your backyard or to be a tournament fly caster, you will need to become a student of the ways of water and of fish and fish foods.

There are two types of fly-fishing water: still water and moving water. Lakes, streams, and oceans have both types. Still water is less common than moving water, even in a lake, because of wind and currents. Oceans have currents, tides, and inflows. In these moving waters, knowledge of casting, presentation, and fly control is important to fly-fishing success. Presenting a fly in calm waters involves casting the fly to a certain spot and then allowing it to rest, or swimming it back toward you. In still water, your fly, leader, and line remain motionless until you move them. The successful fly fisher works the fly at the right depth and with an action that imitates what the fish are feeding on. Drag is no problem on still water unless the wind is blowing. Then you must adjust your retrieving technique as if you were fishing on flowing water.

Achieving good results in moving water requires many casting and presentation techniques. In such waters, at or below the surface, the fly is moving with the water speed and is retrieved across or directly against it.

The natural movements of fish foods range from holding to swimming up, down, or across currents. Imitating such actions with fly tackle is simple. At certain times and places, fish will respond aggressively to a fly fished with an unnatural action. Such reactions, however, are less predictable than are reactions to true imitations of natural fish food.

The fly fisher who prefers to fish moving water should be familiar with three basic fly presentations.

The upstream presentation is one in which the fly is cast upstream to or above the area in which you suspect a fish is waiting. Generally, the upstream presentation allows the fly to float or drift downstream at the speed, and under the control, of the water's flow.

The downstream presentation is one in which the fly is cast downstream just above or to the area that you suspect holds a fish. With this presentation, the fly can be retrieved upstream or—by paying out fly line—allowed to drift downstream.

The across-stream presentation is one in which the fly is cast at an angle across the current to reach or land just above where you suspect a fish is waiting. Variations of the across-stream presentation allow the fly to drift downstream, be retrieved upstream, or be retrieved across stream.

Techniques for Fishing Flies

Artificial flies can deceive fish into mistaking them for the real thing. There are five basic kinds of flies: dry flies, wet flies, nymphs, streamers, and bugs.

Dry flies float on or in the surface to imitate terrestrial or aquatic insects. Generally, such insects float and move with water surface or wind speed and direction. Dry flies are usually presented with a floating fly line and allowed to drift or float as naturally as possible. If the real insect is active on the surface, you should attempt to impart a similar action to the artificial. On the other hand, if the natural is inactive, the imitation should also be inactive. Wind, variable horizontal current speeds, or both of these forces will often cause drag on the fly line, leader, and fly. Drag causes the imitation to move unnaturally. It can usually be avoided by proper presentation and mending of the fly line.

Most dry flies are designed and tied with materials that allow them to float above or in the water's surface film. However, if not treated with a waterproofing agent such as silicone or paraffin, they will soon become wet and sink. This is especially true when a fly has undergone repeated dunkings or has caught many fish. Use a dry-fly spray or paste to waterproof the fly before you use it. Put just enough on to coat the entire fly very lightly. Sprays and liquids are easier to apply, but they are more expensive and do not last as long as the paste dry-fly flotants.

If the dry fly begins to float too low or sink and does not improve after several water-removing false casts, retrieve it and blot it with an absorbent paper or cloth towel or tissue. Absorbing the excess water will help the fly float and will also clean the fly. Apply another coat of dry-fly dressing, and the fly should float like new. The towel is also very useful for cleaning and drying the fly after you remove it—wet, slimy, and matted—from a fish's mouth.

Wet flies sink just below the surface or deeper and generally imitate aquatic insects or small fish swimming, emerging, egg-laying, or drifting helplessly in the water. Wet flies can be fished with floating, sinking-tip, or full-sinking fly lines, depending upon the depth and angle of fish movement. On calm water, wet flies are usually presented on the far side of where you suspect a fish is swimming. The fly is then allowed to sink to the right depth. Then, with whatever action and speed will imitate the natural insect or small minnow, the fly is retrieved to and past the fish. Many wet flies are made in highly colorful attracter patterns, especially those that are used for brook trout, bass, shad, panfish, salmon, and steelhead. These attracter flies are generally fished faster and in a less imitative manner in an attempt to attract and excite the fish.

Wet flies in moving water are generally presented in front of and just above the fish's position. They are drifted or retrieved across or upstream, depending upon what they are designed to imitate and how they are meant to attract or excite the fish. Some wet-fly methods use more than one fly on the leader. (Check regulations for waters you fish.) Sometimes as many as six wet flies are used. These flies are fished in a faster water flow at depths varying from surface to several feet.

Nymphs are designed to be fished below the surface, including on the bottom, of either calm or moving water. Nymphs mainly suggest (give a general impression) or imitate (give a detailed impression) immature aquatic insects. But nymphs also may be used to suggest snails, scuds, leeches, crayfish, worms, and similar foods. Floating, sinking-tip, and full-sinking fly lines are useful in various waters to fish nymphs. For shallow, still, and moving water from one to three feet deep, the floating line is generally best. It allows the best overall fly action and control for nymphing. For medium depth (three to six feet), especially in moving water, the sinking-tip fly line generally works best. For deeper water (6 to 20 feet), either still or moving, a full-sinking line generally performs best with nymphs.

In still waters, the nymph is cast past the fish's swimming path or holding area. It is allowed to sink to the desired depth; then it is retrieved in a method that best suggests the live natural food.

In moving water, nymphs are fished in two basic ways. In the first method they are fished with a floating line and a natural drift. The second way is with a sinking-tip or full-sinking line to achieve a tighter line-to-leader-to-fly contact needed for a swimming action. This method works best when you wish to swim a nymph while retrieving it across or upstream.

Streamers are designed to be fished below the surface to suggest or imitate small fish, minnows, eels, leeches, and so on that are swimming or drifting in the water. Streamers, like nymphs, can be fished with all three fly-line types depending upon the action and the depth desired. The sinking tip is generally the best all-around streamer fly line.

In still waters the streamer is presented past the fish's position and is retrieved past the fish with an action that suggests the natural creature's panic or vulnerability.

In moving water the streamer may be presented at all angles to suggest the natural food's movement. Most naturals are strong swimmers and can live in most areas from top to bottom in a stream. Perhaps the most popular streamer presentation is casting across the current and retrieving with erratic swimming and pausing action as the fly swims and swings down and across the flow. Once the streamer reaches the end of the drift, it is retrieved erratically upstream. Sometimes streamers are effective when cast upstream and allowed to drift motionlessly downstream, as if they were dying or helpless.

Wet flies, nymphs, and streamers perform best when they are tied from soft, water-absorbent materials and after they get wet and take on the natural odors of the waters you fish. Before you begin fishing these three types, rub them on a wet stone, on some aquatic vegetation, or some silt taken from the bottom of the water you plan to fish.

After this simple preparation, they will perform better for you.

Dropper flies (two or more flies) may be used on one leader to increase your chances of catching one or more fish on a cast. (Check regulations first.) Such combinations as two to four wet flies, wet fly and streamer, nymph and streamer, or a dry fly and nymph are often more effective than a single fly. The larger, heavier fly should always be tied to the end of the leader and the smaller, lighter flies tied farther up the leader's tippet. The dropper fly (fly attached to leader's side) is tied on by first tying a blood knot or surgeon's knot with a four- to six-inch tag of heavier tippet material. The fly is then tied on to the long tag with a Duncan loop or improved clinch knot. By using two or three flies at one time on your leader's tip and tippet, you also can efficiently learn what the fish's preference is from repeated catches on one of the flies. Many times two, three, or four flies will also have a violent "emotional" or exciting effect on fish that might ignore a single fly. Casting two or more flies is, however, a bit more difficult than casting one fly.

Bugs float on the surface and suggest larger insects,

Adding One or More Dropper Flies

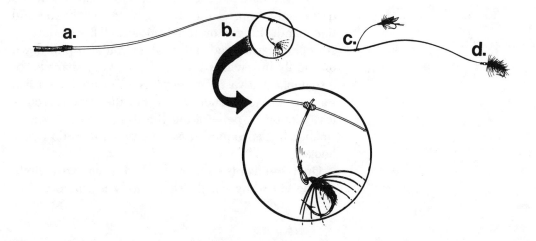

frogs, mice, crippled minnows, and so on. Bugs are fished with a floating or sinking-tip fly line. Use a floating line if bugs are fished just at the surface. A sinking-tip fly line allows them to be fished at the surface, diving, swimming, or surfacing.

For stillwater fishing, bugs are generally presented near or past the fish's location. Often they are most effective when presented near structure such as the bank, lily pads, logs, or overhanging trees. When cast over an object, a bug can be hopped or made to fall into the water to suggest a natural terrestrial food falling into the water. Once on the surface the bug is worked like a miniature puppet, being made to struggle or swim in an attempt to entice a strike. Usually, the slower these types of flies are fished, the more effective they are.

In moving water, bugs are generally cast at all angles and fished with an action similar to what is used in still water. Line drag is avoided by casting-angle adjustments and line mending, as with dry flies. In moving water, bugs are usually fished near or off surface obstructions.

Hooking and Fighting Fish

When you see or feel the fish take your fly, you must be prepared to set the hook quickly. Lack of concentration often prevents strike detection and quick reaction, and the fish detects the fraud and spits out the fly. Practice striking and setting the hook until it becomes a reflex action. This is *very* important! Abundant small panfish such as bluegill or perch are ideal for practice.

To strike and set the hook on most fish requires a quick tightening of the fly line with the fly rod and line hand. Larger or tough-mouthed fish require a stronger, harder rod strike while you also pull down on the fly line with your free hand. Very sharp barbless hooks are vastly more efficient in hooking a fish than are dull or barbed hooks. For the same reason— less friction in penetrating the fish's mouth tissue— smaller hooks require less force to set than do larger hooks.

Once the fish is securely hooked, it will struggle to escape. Landing small fish is rarely a problem. But larger fish have the size and strength to take out line, dive under cover, or break off. Your skill prevents these maneuvers. This is one of the most pleasurable and exciting parts of angling.

Always maintain a taut line on the fish in order to keep the hook embedded and the fish under your control. Know the power of your rod and strength of leader tip. Do not exceed these limits when fighting a large fish. If the fish pulls harder than your tackle can stand, let it pull out line until it tires, slows, or stops. Then resume pulling it in. Another of the great thrills is the feeling you get when you hook a fish that can break off your fly.

Never force a fish in, but rather allow it to jump, swim, and struggle until tired. Likewise, never underplay the fish. Use enough rod and line pressure on it to make it struggle and tire quickly. When fighting a fish in a stream or river, try to position yourself to its side or below it. Fighting a fish upstream will take longer and could give the fish the advantage it needs to get off the hook.

It is a good practice always to fight a fish directly from the reel, rather than strip slack line in or off the reel. Use the rod to pump (or lift up and down), reeling line in when you are letting the rod down. Do not just reel the fish straight in. Using the reel avoids line tangles around you in the water or on objects.

When the hooked fish tires, it will come in swimming slightly on its side. Do not reel it all the way to the rod tip. Always leave the leader outside the rod's tip-top and leave at least a rod length of line and leader between you and the fish. Then the line and leader will have enough stretch to keep from breaking, and the knots will not hang in the guides if the fish makes an unexpected dash.

When the fish is ready to be landed, it will reluctantly but calmly surface and lack the strength to dive away. Depending on its species, size, and location, several methods can be used.

Catch and Release

For various sporting reasons, you may wish to release a fish. It is important for you to know how. To release small fish, if the hook is visible in the fish's mouth, pull the fish close to you. Then simply reach out, grasp the fly, and turn and twist the hook upward. The hook will disengage, and the fish will turn head down and swim away. If the hook is deeper, land the fish by gently sliding your hand under its stomach and lifting it out of the water without squeezing its body. Never put your fingers inside the fish's mouth to free the hook, and try not to lift the fish out of the water. Most fish, even small trout, have sharp teeth or gill rackers that can cause painful or even crippling cuts. Besides, fish are very likely to thrash when they feel your hands. This action can result in your hooking yourself or dropping the fish and injuring it. Use a hook-removal tool, instead. With a hook disgorger or a hemostat, firmly grasp the fly and back the hook out. Quickly place the fish back in the water and give it time to regain its equilibrium and swim out of your hand. When releasing a fish, never *throw* it back into the water. The fish is tired from the fight, and the shock of hitting the water lessens its chances of survival. A small landing net is very useful for landing and releasing small fish.

To release a large fish (16 inches or more), use a landing net or beach it.

When using a net, place the net quietly beneath the water and lead the fish over it. Release most of the tension on the line so that the fish's head will drop, and at the same instant lift the net. Keep most of the net's bag in the water until the fish calms down. Reach inside and unhook the fish, trying to keep the fish's body and gills in the water.

Let the fish revive and swim out of the net bag under its own power. Never dump or toss a fish out.

To beach a large fish, when it surfaces and turns on its side, calmly and gently lead it with steady rod pressure to a gradually sloping shoreline. As the fish beaches itself in the shallows, relax the line pull. Unhook the fish and turn it around, gently coaxing it into deeper water. If the fish is too exhausted to right itself and swim, hold it upright (with your hand near the tail) until it does. Then let it escape your gentle hold under its own power.

If you intend to release the fish, never pull it completely out of the water onto the shore. If you must handle it, do so as tenderly as you would a human infant. Never hold a fish by the gills. Try not to keep an exhausted fish out of the water any longer than you absolutely must.

In any of these cases, if the fish is hooked in the gill or throat, you should cut the leader at the hook eye. The hook will dissolve in time, and the wound will heal. If hooking or hook removal causes continuous bleeding, your fish will most likely die.

If you plan to keep a fish, you should tire it longer before attempting to land it. It is best to use a landing net on freshwater fish such as trout, bass, walleye, pike, and panfish. Most smaller saltwater fish can be landed with a net.

Lead the tired fish with steady, smooth rod pressure over the bag of a still, submerged net. As the fish's head comes over the net's bag, release the rod tension so that its head will begin to sink into the net. At the same time, lift up the net to trap the entire body. Never come down on or from behind a fish with the net; this kind of approach will strike and frighten the fish and cause it to swim or leap away from the net.

Once the fish is in the net and calms down, you may remove the fly hook using the same procedure already described. If the fish is not put in a live well or on a stringer, it is best to kill it immediately. Do this by striking it several times on the top of its head, just behind the eyes, with a small club, or priest.

To beach a fish you wish to kill, *thoroughly tire it out*. Follow the procedure described earlier in catch-and-release beaching except that you should use more force and beach the fish farther up on the shore. Extra tiring will prevent the fish from flopping back in. A sharp rap on the head will stun or kill a thrashing fish.

Many larger freshwater and saltwater fish that you wish to land and keep require the use of either a tailer or a gaff. A tailer is a device that is commonly used by Atlantic-salmon fishermen to disable and hold the salmon with its tail in a loop snare. A gaff is a large metal hook with a sturdy handle for hooking (gaffing) and landing a large fish. The gaff is a more brutal way to land a fish, but it is necessary on strong, large, and dangerous fish such as sharks, billfish, and tuna. It is more difficult to use a gaff or a tailer than to use a net or the beaching method. We do not advise using a gaff or a tailer without personal instruction from an experienced fly fisher or fishing guide.

The priest, actually a fancy club, is used to kill or

Catch and Keep

stun a large fish immediately after it is tailed or gaffed. Strike the fish on the head just behind the eyes. Failure to use a priest can result in personal injury or equipment damage from a large fish thrashing about out of the water.

Tips on Terminal Fly Tackle

Check the fly regularly, especially if it is not drawing strikes or you are missing strikes. Check for a broken hook, dull or bent hook point, moss or weeds on fly, a tangle with the leader, and fly parts wrapped around the hook bend. Also look for any damage that might affect the fly's looks or action.

Check your knots, particularly your fly-to-tippet and tippet-to-tip knots after landing several small or large fish or after extended casting periods. Knots weaken or slip when wet and overtightened.

Check your leader for cuts, abrasions, or wind knots. Replace tippet if it has wind knot or abrasions. Failure to do so will surely cause loss of fly or fly and fish.

Check leader for twists or curls, and straighten them by stroking the leader tight with your fingers and palm. Twists or curls cause the fly to cast poorly and land off target.

Check for fly-line tangles on or around the fly reel as well as around the rod between guides.

Check to see if rod's ferrule is tight, if guides are lined up, and if the reel is still tight on the handle. Do these checks at least twice a day.

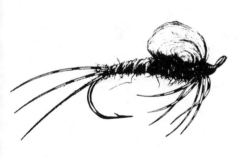

Common Fly-Fishing Problems and Solutions

Problem: Scaring fish. This is a problem most fly fishers encounter until they recognize that fish are frightened by their presence and noise as well as the disturbance made in fly-casting and presentation.

Solution: Stay low, move slowly and quietly, and wear clothes that do not contrast with the background. Try to cast so that your rod and line are not easily visible to the fish. Make your presentation softly, and keep your fly line and leader from splashing or floating over a fish.

Problem: Missing strikes.

Solution: Keep your fly hooks extremely sharp and stay *constantly alert*. Be ready the instant a fish takes the fly. Avoid excessive slack line. Practice striking quickly. Also regularly check to see if your hook point is dulled or broken from striking stones on your backcast. Polarizing sunglasses are a great aid in seeing strikes and fish.

Problem: Breaking off fish on the strike.

Solution: Use less force when you strike, and make sure your hooks are very sharp. Do not strike harder on a large fish than is needed to set the hook on a similar but smaller fish. Also, you might increase the strength of your leader tippet if break-offs persist. Tie your knots very carefully, and test them before fishing the fly. Check your tippet for wind knots regularly.

Problem: Hooks breaking. This is a common problem for beginners and experts alike. It occurs when the fly is allowed to drop and strike stones on the backcast.

Solution: Keep your backcast power stroke higher, and use a bit more power to keep the cast up. Sometimes the hooks will break on hooked fish; this happens because of poor hook quality or, more likely, because of improper placement and excess tightening in a fly-tying vise.

Problem: Dry flies float poorly or sink.

Solution: If dry flies are properly constructed and waterproofed, they should float well. You may be presenting the fly too hard and thus it is dunked on impact. Make sure the fly is well waterproofed with dry-fly spray or paste. Drop it to the water with presentation about two feet above the water so it will light softly. When you pick it up, make one or two quick, brisk false casts to shake the water out of it. This tactic does not necessarily dry it completely but reduces its weight so it will light softly again on the next presentation. After you catch a fish on the fly, blot off the slime and water with a soft paper towel, a chamois, or a tissue before casting it again.

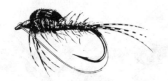

Problem: Dry flies dragging and scaring rising fish. When a dry fly moves across, up, or down the current unnaturally, it is dragging and will often scare a rising fish.

Solution: Make your presentation with more slack leader and line, and learn to mend a surface line that is moving faster or slower than the fly.

Problem: Line and fly won't come off the water easily. This results from your floating line sinking. When your floating fly line sinks a bit, it has usually been coated with particles of dirt.

Solution: Clean your fly line with a damp cloth or soapy rag. Wipe line dry and apply some fly-line flotant or polish. Fly will float higher and pick up much easier. You might also practice lifting the fly line out of the water slower and more smoothly.

Problem: Fly goes too deep and hangs up on the bottom. When your fly goes too deep, it will hook on various objects.

Solution: In still water, do not allow the fly to sink so long. Retrieve a bit faster. In flowing water, cast the fly with a little less angle upstream or start your retrieve sooner.

Problem: Sinking fly lines and heavily weighted flies are difficult to pick up.

Solutions: Pull more of the line in past your rod's tip-top and use a short roll cast to lift the remainder. As the roll reaches the line's tip, initiate a regular pickup to begin your backcast. This procedure will work well for any type of fly that is difficult to pick up.

Reading Water

Reading water begins with the choice of what water to fish and when. All fish are coldblooded and must live and feed according to season, weather, water temperature, and water volume. You should learn the seasonal requirements of fish in the waters you plan to fish.

Once you are on the water, there are several ways you can read water. First you must learn to recognize the overall structure of any area of a lake, stream, canal, bay, or ocean. Structure is what lies along the perimeter, on the bottom, and extends up from or down to the bottom. Structure may be rocks, moss beds, fallen trees, or other such objects. It is around these structures that fish live. Food is more plentiful here, and the structure provides protection from predators. Eddies and pools created by structure provide relief from strong currents. Spawning often takes place in these same fertile protected areas. To find fish, learn to recognize major structure areas.

The fly fisher should understand that clear water looks darker with an increase in depth. Depth and bottom structures fill most of the needs of fish. Polarizing sunglasses are a great aid to you in seeing through the reflective water surface. If fish are not clearly visible at the surface or in the shallow water, they most likely will be hidden in the deeper, darker water. Since fish often have camouflage coloration, they will not be easy to see. Watch for their movements and shadows on the bottom.

In streams, the water's surface tells how fast the water is moving and what structure might lie unseen in the murky or darker water. A large underwater boulder or log, for example, will cause surface irregularities. Flowing water usually moves fastest at the surface and slowest at the bottom. In streams, fish are usually found during feeding periods in moderate riffles, pocket waters, and runs, along the shoreline of pools, on flats, or in the pool tails. When they are resting or in nonfeeding periods, you may still entice strikes by fishing in deep pocket water, slower riffles, and runs, and down a pool's channel. Entering spring

Fresh-Water Lake: Typical Structures and Probable Fish Locations

Code:
a. shorelines
b. inlet
c. outlet
d. main channel
e. neck
f. points
g. flats
h. cove
i. dam dike
j. spring

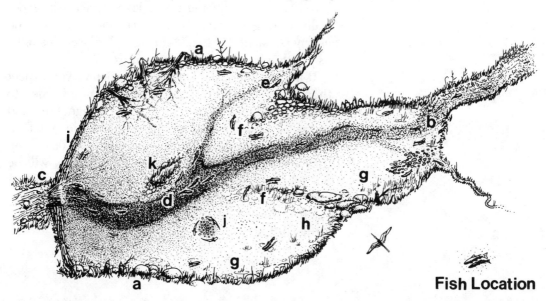

Fish Location

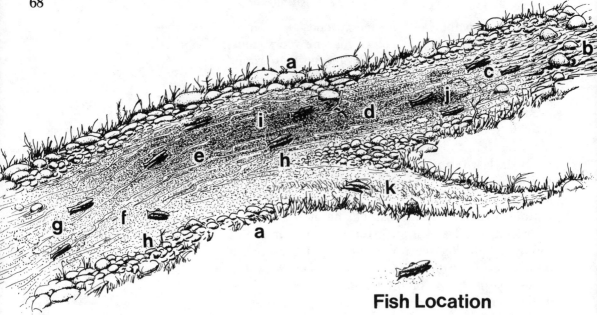

Fish Location

Fresh-Water Stream: Typical Structures and Probable Fish Locations

Code:
a. banks
b. rapid
c. riffle
d. run
e. pool
f. flats
g. tail
h. bars
i. main channel
j. pocket water
k. slough

water can attract fish in streams as it does in lakes.

Reading water, therefore, involves seeing fish or identifying areas that are likely to hold fish. Good water reading can save hours of unproductive fishing.

In lakes, fish are usually found feeding at inlets along weedy or rocky shorelines, over and around offshore weedbeds, just off points, and up in coves. If the wind is blowing, they usually feed beneath the surface on the downwind side and on the surface on the upwind side. During nonfeeding periods, you catch fish in the deeper channels by fishing your fly deep or near bottom. Natural springs seeping up from lake bottoms or flowing into a lake attract fish, especially during very cold and very hot weather. The nearly constant 45° to 55° spring water provides most fish with a comfortable temperature.

If fish do not strike your flies as soon as you expect them to, have patience and keep your mind tuned to reading and studying the water. Change flies and methods, and try different areas. Fish do not feed constantly, and there will be periods each day when they seem asleep and other times when they will be outright aggressive. The angler often finds his greatest satisfaction and pleasure in using his skill and wit to catch the fish that is the most reluctant to take the artificial fly.

4

Natural Foods for Fish

Wherever fish live, there is a natural food chain. Knowing food sources, imitating them with flies, and fishing them to fool and catch fish are the signs of a good fly fisher. A basic knowledge of streams, lakes, marshes, estuaries, oceans, and the fish foods they hold is important.

Unpolluted freshwater streams and lakes usually produce abundant fish foods. The major fish foods are aquatic insects, small fish, crustaceans, terrestrial insects and other invertebrates, and aquatic plants.

Aquatic Insects

Aquatic insects live a major part of their life cycles underwater. Their life cycles are generally one year, but in some groups life cycles are as short as two months or as long as four years. These insects provide fish with year-round opportunity to feed on the immature nymph forms and the adults. Because of their abundance and vulnerability, they are often favored by fish such as trout, bass, or panfish, and are important for the fly fisher to imitate. They are seldom important in saltwater fishing.

The most abundant aquatic insects are mayflies, caddisflies, stoneflies, midges, damselflies, and dragonflies. The life cycle for these insects includes an aquatic nymph stage, which emerges on the water's surface and hatches into a winged adult insect. These adults, which live only a few hours or days, mate and lay their eggs on the water before dying.

It was the desire to imitate these aquatic insects that initially stimulated fly-fishing. A large number of standard fly designs are imitations of aquatic insects.

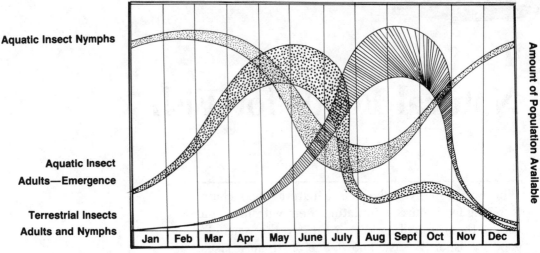

Peak

Aquatic Insect Nymphs

Aquatic Insect
Adults—Emergence

Terrestrial Insects
Adults and Nymphs

| Jan | Feb | Mar | Apr | May | June | July | Aug | Sept | Oct | Nov | Dec |

Amount of Population Available

Low

Abundance Cycles of Aquatic and Terrestrial Insects
(Width of Bars Indicates Relative Size of Insect)

INSECT SIZE AND SEASON

Aquatic Insects: January to March, small sizes (18 to 26) of midges, mayflies, caddisflies and stoneflies. March to June, small to medium sizes (12 to 18) of mayflies, caddisflies, midges, and stoneflies. June to August, large and small sizes of caddisflies, mayflies, damselflies, stoneflies, midges, and dragonflies (size 4 to 24). August to October, small and medium sizes (16 to 24) of mayflies, caddisflies and midges. October to December, small sizes (18 to 26) of midges, mayflies, and caddisflies.

Terrestrial Insects: Generally in small sizes (16 to 18) beginning around April, increasing in variety of sizes steadily to early September, then decreasing in number but not size until fall and winter freezes. The crawling ants and gnats are first to appear in spring. Crawling and flying ants, moths, bees, flies, small and large beetles, inchworms, spiders, small crickets, and grasshoppers appear from late spring to midsummer. Flying and crawling ants, small beetles, various sizes of grasshoppers and crickets, leafhoppers, spiders, bees, wasps, caterpillars, and spiders from late summer until the first frost of fall.

Note: Aquatic adult insects and immature and adult terrestrial insects are most frequently imitated by floating flies. Immature aquatic insects (nymphs, larvae, pupae) are generally imitated by sinking flies.

Matching and fishing aquatic insects is still the most captivating method of fly-fishing for trout, grayling, char, bass, and panfish.

MAYFLIES (Ephemeroptera) are a large, very important group of delicate aquatic insects that live in streams and lakes. The life cycle consists of egg, nymph, and adult stages. The nymph, which feeds and grows beneath the surface from periods of a few months to a year or two years, swims to the surface when mature and hatches into the first adult stage, the dun. The winged dun, an air breather, flies off the water's surface, leaving its nymphal skin behind. It conceals itself in the waterside terrestrial structures (trees, weeds, rocks, or bushes). The dun, after 10 to 20 hours, sheds another skin and changes into the sexually mature adult stage called the spinner. Spinners fly near or over the water and mate in the air, and the females lay their eggs on or below the surface. Both males and females die shortly after this activity.

Natural Aquatic Insects and Fly Imitations

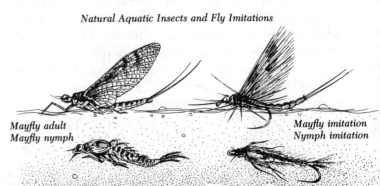

Mayfly adult
Mayfly nymph

Mayfly imitation
Nymph imitation

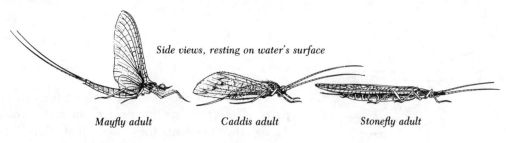

Side views, resting on water's surface

Mayfly adult *Caddis adult* *Stonefly adult*

An adult is most recognizable by its large, upright, sail-shaped wings (at rest); long, round, slender, tapering body; and two or three very long, delicate tails.

Mayfly nymphs generally live one year. Mayfly nymphs vary greatly in size, color, and shape depending on species and age. All have six legs, two or three tails and sets of gills on the sides and top of the body.

STONEFLIES (Plecoptera) are aquatic insects that are generally large and live in very pure, well-aereated streams. They have a life cycle very similar to that of mayflies. The adult is best identified by two large pairs of wings, which at rest are folded or rolled around the top sides of the body, giving the insect an almost stick-like appearance. It has two distinctive, large antennae and two distinctive tails, very widely separated.

Nymphs vary widely in size, color, and shape, according to species and age. Nymphs are best identified by their two distinctive wing cases (pads), two tails and antennae, and a fuzzy, light-colored gill filament under and between their six legs.

CADDISFLIES (Trichoptera) are very large, widely distributed, mothlike, lake and stream insects. They have a four-stage life cycle: egg, larva, pupa, and adult. The life cycle generally lasts one year. From the egg, a larva is produced. This grubwormlike larva lives at the bottom of the water. Many species of caddisfly larva construct a case in which they live. These cases are made uniquely according to species from glue and a silklike filament in combination with

Midge adult

Four Major Aquatic Insects That Fish Most Often Eat and Flyfishers Imitate with Flies

Midge pupa

Top

Side

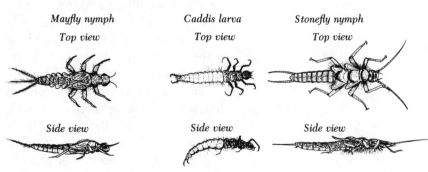

Mayfly nymph *Caddis larva* *Stonefly nymph*
Top view *Top view* *Top view*

Side view *Side view* *Side view*

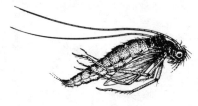

Caddis pupa

Three Common Forms of Cased Caddis Larvae

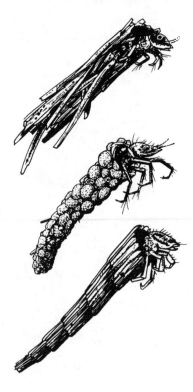

aquatic plant pieces, sand grains, or terrestrial plant parts. The cases are for protection and camouflage. Along the bottom, they look like short sticklike structures.

The larva develops into the third stage, the pupa, which is very similar to the cocoon of a butterfly or moth. The larva seals its case to begin pupation. This stage generally lasts a few weeks. Then the pupa, now very different physically from the larva, cuts out of its case, swims, rises, or crawls to the surface, and hatches into the adult caddisfly.

Adults live several days to several weeks, during which time they mate and lay eggs on or below the water's surface.

Adults are best distinguished from the three other major aquatic insects discussed by their tentlike or mothlike wing shape when at rest. Many appear opaque, fuzzy, mottled, and heavily veined. Caddisflies have two very long antennae and no distinctive tails on a modestly sized body.

The larva has a rather bare, light-colored abdomen with some gill filaments on its lower side. It has no visible wing pads on its darker thorax and no visible antennae or tails.

The pupa has six long, skinny legs, wing pads at the side or lower part of its midsection (thorax) and two very distinctive antennae. A good way to study pupae is to pick their sealed cases off the bottom structures, and open to remove the developing insect.

MIDGES (Diptera). This is very widely distributed and immensely abundant group of aquatic insects. Midges have a very similar but usually shorter life cycle than caddisflies. They are generally very small insects, seldom exceeding one-quarter inch in length.

The mosquitolike midge adult is identified by its one pair of wings, smaller than its body and positioned flat and to each side of the body at rest. It has three pairs of legs, which are very long and skinny. Males have two very large, plum-like antennae, but no tails.

The larvae are very simple, slender, segmented worms with no distinctively clear head, body, or tail. The pupae are similar in color to the larvae but have a much fatter head-thorax section. Close magnification will show gill plumes on head and tail and folded legs and wings under the head-thorax section.

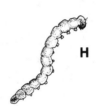
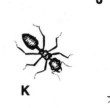

Terrestrial Insects Important to Imitate
A. Spider; B.-F. Assorted Beetles; G. Caterpillar; H. Inch-
worm I.-K. Ants; L. Leafhopper (Jassid); M. Cricket;
N. Grasshopper (immature); N. Grasshopper

Terrestrial Insects

Terrestrial insects—those insects that are born and spend their immature and mature stages on land—are a second major insect food source for many freshwater fish. This is especially so in warmer latitudes and, through the summer months, in colder parts of North America.

Fish feed on terrestrial insects that accidentally fall on the water during flight, during mating swarms, or from overhanging plants. Wind, rain, cold snaps, floods, drought, crop harvesting, and similar activities often create conditions that force terrestrial insects to become water trapped. Some sink slowly, but most will float low in the water's surface film. Most terrestrial fly imitations are floating designs.

The important terrestrial insects to imitate are ants, beetles, grasshoppers, leafhoppers, crickets, caterpillars (worms), wasps, moths, bees, and spiders. Terrestrial insects usually become more abundant and larger when aquatic insects decline in numbers and slow down in activity.

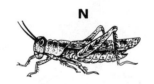

Crustaceans

This is an important large group of natural aquatic fish foods that are similar to both aquatic insects and fish

Three Important Crustaceans

Scud (freshwater shrimp)

Sowbug

Crayfish

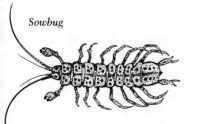
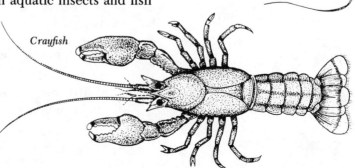

in their movements, shapes, and habits. They are widely distributed. The most important crustaceans for the freshwater fly fisherman to imitate are scuds (freshwater shrimp), sowbugs, and crayfish. All three of these crawl along the bottom structures of lakes and streams. The scud and crayfish can swim erratically and rapidly backward if fleeing from a fish.

Saltwater crustaceans important to imitate are crabs, shrimp, scuds, and crayfish. Each of these can crawl and swim.

All species have a simple life cycle lasting one to several years, in which they seasonally increase in size while the population decreases because of predation. Like most other coldblooded creatures, crustaceans are most active and most abundant during the milder seasons. They are imitated by nymphs, wet flies, and modified streamer designs. In still water, cast the imitation, allow it to sink nearly to the bottom, and strip it back toward you. In flowing water, strip it downstream to you.

Other Invertebrates

Aquatic leeches, snails, and worms make up an assortment of fish foods that varies in importance depending on their abundance compared to the other major foods already described. Knowledge of their existence, life cycles, actions, sizes, and colors will—if imitated and fished properly—enable the fly fisher to make good catches.

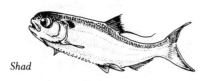

Shad

Minnows

Minnow is the name used by fishermen to indicate mature small fish or immature large fish that other fish feed on. Minnows are sometimes called forage fish. Like aquatic insects, they are important and abundant fish foods in fresh water. Minnows are extremely important in salt water.

Their life cycles, usually several years long, expose them daily to predator fish that ambush, chase, and eat them. Minnows are imitated by streamers.

Fish eat a wide range of minnows. Generally, practical fly-fishing sizes are one-half to eight inches long. They vary from natural colors to bright attracter colors. Minnows are found in all areas from top to bottom, but usually choose an area specific to their species. For example, shad and shiners live in clear, open water, chub and dace near underwater structures, and sculpin and suckers on the bottom.

Chub

Minnow imitations are usually fished to imitate panic or distress. This action suggests vulnerability and stimulates attack by predator fish.

Sculpin

The Ecology of Fisheries

Food chain is the term used to describe the sequence of feeding from the simple plants and animals through the most complex forms. Each more complex form feeds upon the lesser forms. The least complex forms feed on the decomposing matter of the higher forms, thus completing the endless food chain. The experienced fly fisher recognizes an excellent fishery by the food chain. Waters lacking a good food chain will provide poor fishing or no fishing. If fishing is poor or changes from excellent to poor, it is a strong indication of larger problems in the environment.

As a sportsman, you have an obligation to look after the environment. You may do so by picking up litter, taking care not to damage shore and bottom, reporting pollution, cooperating with landowners, writing letters to support important wildlife management projects, donating to wildlife causes, or releasing fish. Such investments will bring great dividends to you and future generations.

5

Fly-Fishing Apparel and Accessories

Fly-fishing, being an on-the-water, all-season outdoor sport, requires certain apparel and accessories to provide comfort, efficiency, and safety.

Clothing. No matter what season or weather you fly-fish in, you will function best if your clothes are light as conditions allow, loose, comfortable, and non-binding. They should be functional, not fancy or stylish. Choose clothes that breathe and give you protection against sun, wind, dampness, and insects. For practicality, avoid non-washable fabrics. To avoid being seen by fish, choose subtle natural colors.

Fishing hats. The ideal hat for fly-fishing should have a good visor and brim to give your head and neck protection from sun, wind, and insects. It should be reasonably rainproof and fit snugly enough so that the wind will not blow it off. Under certain conditions, you may want a hat that will accommodate a bug net. A fringe benefit of wearing a hat is that it protects you from getting hooked in the head.

Rain and wind jackets. The most practical jacket for wading should fold into a small bundle and fit inside your fishing-vest back pocket or your wader pouch. For wading, it should not go below your waist. It should have a hood that will comfortably fit over your head and hat. Drawstrings at the hood and waist, and snug wristbands help keep out rain and wind. Be sure your jacket will fit over your normal outerwear, including fishing vest. Do not waste your money on jackets that are made from plastic that hardens or stiffens in cold weather.

If you intend to fish without waders from shore or from a boat, your jacket should extend at least below your hips for ample protection.

Fishing vests. For fly-fishing on foot, a fishing vest is extremely useful. It should contain enough well-designed pockets to carry what you will need for a day's fishing. This includes fly boxes, rain jacket, sunglasses, film, and so on. Choose a lightweight model without too many pockets. Shortie style vests are most practical for the fly fisher who wades fairly deep. If you are a nonswimmer or you regularly wade treacherous, deep water, a flotation fishing vest is strongly recommended. When fishing from shore or a boat, you may choose to use a tackle box instead of a vest.

Waders. For cold-water wading, chest-high waders are a necessity. There are two designs: the stocking-foot wader and the boot-foot wader.

Stocking-foot waders are more portable and lightweight; they allow more freedom of movement. They are better for getting in and out of boats and float-planes, for backpacking in, and for float-tube fishing. You must wear socks and good, sturdy wading shoes over the feet.

Boot-foot waders are generally more durable, heavier, and warmer but restrict leg movement more. These waders are faster and easier to put on and take off, as the shoe or boot is part of them. When the fishing is easily accessible, boot-foot waders are a better overall choice for the fly fisher.

If you plan to fish in colder weather and wade deep, cold water, and you have no weight-load problems, then insulated waders are ideal. Lightweight waders are less durable but more portable and less tiring to wear. In very cold conditions, extra underwear and stocking insulation can be worn.

Wader boots, like hiking boots, should give you protection against ankle and foot bruise and sprain. More importantly they should give good bottom traction. There are three general types of boot soles:

Rubber cleats are best for soft mud and clay and sand bottoms but very dangerous on slick bedrock or rubble rock bottoms.

Felt soles are good for hard bedrock and rubble rock bottoms where there is excessively swift water or

very slick algae. Felt soles are poor for mud, sand, or clay bottoms.

Soft-metal cleat soles are ideal for hard bedrock or large rubble bottoms that are very slick or in very swift water. They are fair to good for soft bottom wading. Metal cleats are impractical, however, for wearing in boats or rafts or on dry rock.

Felt or metal-cleat wading sandals, which fit over either wading shoes or the boots of waders, are very convenient when you want to convert quickly and simply from one sole to another.

Wader suspenders, belts, and patch kits are absolutely necessary for efficient and safe water use.

Hip-high wading boots are a popular, convenient, comfortable means of fishing from shorelines and wading shallow water. Do not use them for boat wear or wading areas over your knees. If you go in too deep, they quickly fill with water and will disable your legs.

Wader belts and wading staffs are two important safety items. The snug wader belt will take part of the wader weight off your shoulders, but more importantly it will keep your waders from filling with water if you fall or go into water that's too deep. The wading staff is a third leg while you wade slick or swift water or test the depth ahead of you. It also helps you negotiate stream shorelines or steep trails.

Useful Fly-Fishing Accessories

Polarized sunglasses— a must for fly-fishing	Compass
	Band-aids
Wading staff	Matches (waterproof) or butane lighter
Creel	
Clippers	Small whistle
Hook sharpener	Folding cup
Scissors-pliers	Insect repellent
Leader wallet	Small knife
Fly boxes	Patch kit
Fly flotant	Lip balm
Fly-line dressing	Hemostat
Paper towels	Thermometer
Leader-tippet spools	Small aquarium net

6
Fish Made for Fly-Fishing

Fly-fishing complemented by innovative and creative fly-tying is a method that provides almost limitless opportunity to catch any species of fish. Identify the fish, determine what it eats or will strike, and where, how, and when it will strike. Then deceive the fish into accepting the fly. Some fish, such as trout, salmon, bass, and bonefish, are classic fly-fishing quarry called gamefish. Others are thought to be lesser sport. This is an arbitrary classification, and you will be better off making your own judgments here.

TROUT (Trout Family). Trout are widely distributed cold-water stream and lake fish that are the most traditional and popular fly-fishing quarry. In fact, trout probably are the main reason fly-fishing was first conceived, and they have been the fish most sought after by fly fishers. The most common and popular species are rainbow trout, brown trout, cutthroat trout, and (more rare) golden trout. (The brook trout is actually a char, and it is dealt with in a later section.)

Unpolluted freshwater streams and lakes that have average summertime temperatures of 50° to 60° and seldom reach 70° will most likely have trout living in them. Trout are beautifully colored strong fish. They feed on a wide variety of natural foods. They can be enticed to strike many natural or attracter patterned flies. They feed most actively in rising or stable water temperatures of 50° to 60°. They feed principally

Rainbow Trout

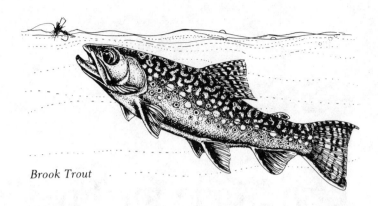

Brook Trout

by sight, either on or below the surface. Most prefer to eat live small insects, crustaceans, and minnows. There are many popular fly designs to imitate these foods.

Trout average 8 to 12 inches (half-pound) but 15- to 28-inch (two to eight pounds) fish are regularly caught on flies. Trout are excellent eating, but kills should be limited in the interest of conservation. Trout that are released properly may live to be caught again, providing anglers more pleasure. Or they may spawn and provide the valuable breeding stock necessary to ensure future fishing.

Brown Trout

CHAR (Trout Family). Char are a widely distributed group of troutlike fish that inhabit cold and very cold waters of North America. Even more so than trout, they require very clean, clear, and cold lake or stream environments. Char are beautiful, vividly colored, strong, aggressive, and active fish. They feed on aquatic insects, minnows, and crustaceans, and are generally thought to be more gullible than trout. Char prefer to feed in water of 40° to 55°.

The most popular species of true char are brook trout, arctic char, Dolly Varden, lake trout, and Sunapee trout. The splake is a hybrid char of brook- and lake-trout cross. Brook trout are much more like true trout in their ranges and habits than other char. The other char are larger water, deeper feeding, minnow eaters in general, so minnow imitations are best. Char that will hit flies range widely in size from eight inches to 20 pounds. The deep, cold-water-loving lake trout often runs larger. They are not, however, the best char for fly-fishing, because they are usually found very deep in a lake and are hard to reach by casting flies. All are excellent eating, but should, like trout, be harvested sparingly.

GRAYLING (Trout Family). A beautiful, delicate, relatively rare, troutlike cold-water fish highly prized by North American fly fishers, grayling have a distinctive, large, sailfishlike dorsal fin. They require very pure, cold, clear, lake or stream water. Most good grayling fishing is found in the Montana and Wyoming Rockies and in northwestern Canada and Alaska. Grayling feed predominately on active insects but will also feed on crustaceans and small minnows. Smaller flies, especially dry flies, are most effective.

Grayling average 8 to 14 inches but grow as large as four pounds, especially in Alaska. They prefer to feed in water of 45° to 55°. Grayling are active but not powerful fighters.

LANDLOCK SALMON (Trout Family). Landlocks are believed by many authorities to have evolved from Atlantic salmon that were landlocked, perhaps thousands of years ago. They are somewhat smaller than ocean salmon but every bit as beautiful, streamlined, fast, and hard-fighting. Landlocks occur naturally in the rivers and lakes of Maine and southeastern Canada and have been successfully introduced to a few other Northeastern states and other sections of Canada, as well as South America. They feed principally on minnows and aquatic insects and are aggressive surface and subsurface fly strikers.

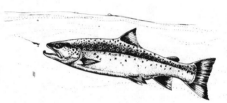

Landlocked Salmon

ATLANTIC SALMON (Trout Family). On the Atlantic Coast, only the Atlantic salmon is native, and it is second only to trout in traditional popularity with fly fishermen. In fact, in North American rivers, sport-fishing is limited to flies to catch these magnificent fish as they enter the rivers from May to October to spawn. Though Atlantic salmon are thought not to feed once they return to fresh water to spawn, they strike wet, dry, and streamer salmon flies very well. Salmon range from three to eight pounds (grilse) and nine to forty pounds for mature salmon. They are superb eating but should be killed sparingly, for their stocks are threatened.

Atlantic Salmon

Pacific Sockeye Salmon

PACIFIC SALMON (Trout Family). There are four abundant species of Pacific salmon: chinook (or king), coho, sockeye, and chum (or pink). They are fine gamefish, but less popular with the traditional cold-water fly fisher than trout, Atlantic salmon, or char. Pacific salmon spawn once and die, whereas the Atlantic salmon may spawn more than once during its lifetime. Neither type of salmon eats once it returns to fresh water to spawn but will strike a wide variety of surface and subsurface attracter flies. All salmon are strong fighters and are considered superb eating. They average from three to ten pounds for chum or sockeye, and twelve to forty for coho or chinook. Some chinook exceed sixty pounds. In the past few decades, many Pacific salmon and some Atlantic salmon have been successfully introduced to larger freshwater lake systems, such as the Great Lakes in the United States and Canada.

STEELHEAD (Trout Family). The steelhead is a unique rainbow trout that has adapted to a sea or large lake residence like salmon, and requires a temporary spawning run into connecting rivers. Then it returns to the ocean or lake. Steelhead are equaled only by Atlantic salmon as large, strong, high-leaping, long-running, freshwater fly-caught fish. They are most abundant in the coastal rivers of California to Alaska and in the Great Lakes. Steelhead average four to eight pounds and often exceed twenty pounds in these areas. They do feed a little during their upstream and downstream migrations and will strike both natural and attracter surface and subsurface flies.

Sea trout, or Costers, are names often used for trout that live in the sea, and, like salmon and steelhead, swim up connecting rivers to spawn. Most common are brown trout, cutthroat, and chars (brook trout and

Dolly Varden). Because of their sea vitality, all are significantly stronger than their resident freshwater counterparts.

BASS (Sunfish Family). Bass are found in warm and cool water. They are strong and aggressive and willing to take a fly. They prefer freshwater and brackish-water lakes and slower streams that are relatively unpolluted and have an average summer temperature range of 65° to 80°. Most North American fresh waters that are not trout fisheries will be bass fisheries.

Bass feed aggressively on all types of insects, crustaceans, minnows, amphibians, reptiles, and mammals. They are less selective and generally prefer larger foods than do trout. Bass can be solitary or found in small, loose schools. They prefer to ambush live surface and subsurface foods along the shorelines or near open-water structures such as large boulders, aquatic plants, fallen trees, or boat docks. They feed most actively in rising or stable water temperatures of 55° to 80°.

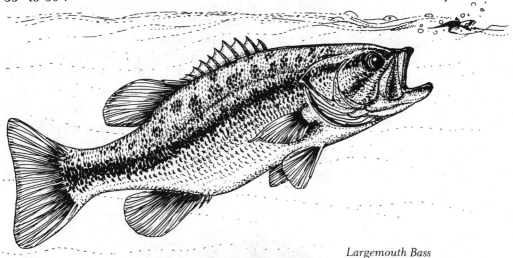

Largemouth Bass

There are three popular species of bass: small-mouth, largemouth, and spotted (Kentucky) bass. They average about one pound or 12 inches, but it is not unusual to catch two- to ten-pound bass on flies. Smallmouth bass are closer to trout in their habitat preference, inhabiting cooler water. They are generally more popular with fly fishers. The spotted and largemouth bass, however, are also fine fly-rod fish. All three strike hard, jump frequently, and fight a

Smallmouth Bass

strong close-quarters battle. Bass are good to eat, but like trout should be taken and killed in limited numbers to ensure good fishing in future seasons.

BLUEGILL (Sunfish Family). Bluegill are the most popular and abundant panfish in North America's cool and warm waters. They normally inhabit the same waters as bass, but in far greater numbers. They are sassy, quick, strong, and very aggressive. They feed on or below the surface on live or dead insects, crustaceans, and minnows. They are sight feeders. Their small size and tiny mouths make it necessary for them to feed mostly on small foods. Flies from size 6 to 16, or one to one-half inch long, are best.

Similar sunfish, such as red ear, green sunfish, rock bass, and pumpkinseed usually inhabit the same waters as the bluegill. All will strike similar flies and, like the bluegill, they are usually very abundant and good to eat. Most average five to six inches in length and occasionally grow to one pound or more. They are wonderful and convenient fish for practicing fly-fishing.

Bluegill

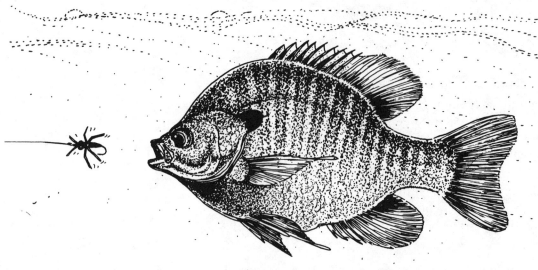

CRAPPIE (Sunfish Family). A very abundant and widely distributed cool- and warm-water panfish, the crappie is usually present in the same waters as bass and bluegill, but generally prefers deeper, calmer water. Crappie are school fish that feed aggressively subsurface on small minnows, aquatic insects, and some crustaceans. They are usually found hiding and feeding beside and under various submerged structures, such as weed beds, reeds, dead trees, boat docks, or rock ledges. Crappie are both daytime and nighttime feeders.

Crappie

There are two crappie species: white and black. The white crappie is generally more abundant in the South and Midwest and is a bit larger than the black. Blacks strike a fly more aggressively, fight a bit more, and do not form such large schools. Crappie average about eight inches long and one-half pound to a pound. But specimens are regularly caught, especially during shallow-water spawning, that weigh up to 2½ pounds. They have firm, flaky, white, delicious flesh. Like most other panfish, they are so abundant that keeping them usually helps future fishing.

WHITE BASS (Perch Family). White bass are an extremely abundant school panfish found in warm, cool, and cold waters. They prefer larger lakes and rivers rich with various minnows. White bass move almost constantly, feeding on minnows at all depths. They are aggressive and will strike streamers and top-water bugs. They fight extremely hard for their size, which averages about ¾ of a pound to 2½ pounds. White bass are very good to eat.

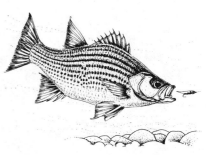

White Bass

YELLOW PERCH (Perch Family). A relatively abundant cool-water panfish, yellow perch prefer lakes but also inhabit some streams that usually are considered bass waters. They prefer to feed on subsurface and bottom aquatic insects, crustaceans,

Yellow Perch

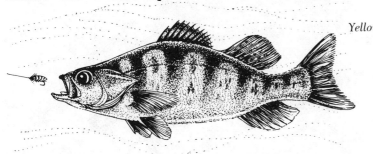

worms, and small minnows. They strike best on small flies fished slow and deep. Perch average about 10 inches (one-half pound) and some run as large as two pounds. They have a fine, firm, white flesh excellent for eating. They are fun to catch but are not particularly spectacular fighters.

WALLEYED PIKE (Perch Family). Walleyes are very popular cool- to cold-water school fish. They are widely distributed, living in clean, hard-bottom, deep lakes and streams. Much like the crappie they make up in eating quality and beauty for what they lack in hard-fighting character. Most are subsurface fly strikers. Walleyes are predominantly minnow feeders but occasionally feed on aquatic insects, amphibians, crustaceans, and worms. Walleyes average about one pound but three- to seven-pound fly-caught walleyes are not uncommon. They have very firm, flaky, white meat that is delicious.

NORTHERN PIKE (Pike Family). Pike are fairly widely distributed cool- and cold-water lake and stream fish that are found mostly in the northern United States, Canada, and southern Alaska. They are strong, very aggressive fish that prefer to ambush their food from near shore and bottom structures. They feed mostly on other fish, amphibians, crustaceans, mammals, and birds in water of 45° to 65° F. As fly-rod fish, there has not been nearly enough said— they are truly as exciting or more so than bass or trout.

Pike are alligatorlike in appearance, and that may discourage some fly fishers from appreciating them. They are frequently caught accidentally on bass flies or large trout flies. They average 20 inches and about three pounds, but often weigh as much as fifteen pounds. They are bony, but good eating.

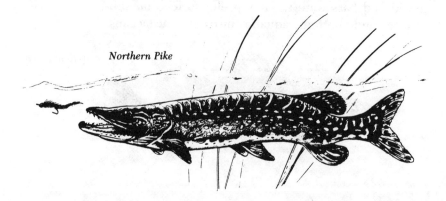

Northern Pike

MUSKELLUNGE (Pike Family). Large, pikelike fish that are less widely distributed than northern pike but live in the same lake or stream conditions, muskie are rarely caught on flies. However, they present a great challenge to the fly fisher because of their very large size (eight to twenty-five pounds), high intelligence, and fighting qualities. A stream muskie over 30 inches caught on a top-water fly is probably a more rare fly-rod trophy than any other freshwater gamefish.

CHAIN PICKEREL (Pike Family). This is a smaller pikelike fish in the same family as pike and muskie. Chain pickerel are much more widespread in streams and lakes of the East and South, and they are very fast, vicious, hard-striking, surface and subsurface ambush feeders. They feed on minnows, amphibians, and small mammals. They average 12 to 18 inches, and occasionally two- to six-pounders are caught on flies. Most successful bass flies work equally well for pickerel. They are very bony but are delicious.

Chain Pickerel

SHAD (Herring Family). An abundant group of delicate, silver, deep-bodied school fish, shad principally prefer cool to warm fresh, brackish, and salt waters. Most of these fish, including hickory shad, gizzard shad, American shad, skipjacks, and golden eye, strike attracter flies during their spring spawning runs up streams that flow into larger rivers, lakes, and oceans.

These fish are fast, strong fighters and generally willing leapers that run from about one to three pounds up to five or six pounds. They vary in eating quality.

CARP (Minnow Family). Carp are abundant, hardy scavenger fish that live in warm or cool waters. They will readily take flies that closely imitate their preferred natural foods of aquatic insects, aquatic worms, terrestrial plants, tree seeds or fruits, and aquatic vegetation. Carp average 3 to 8 pounds and often exceed 20 pounds. Their careful, slow foraging on the surface and the bottom of lakes and sluggish streams, with their small, sensitive mouths, makes them a real test for the fly fisher. Once hooked, they are beastly strong and stubborn fighters. Only fair eating.

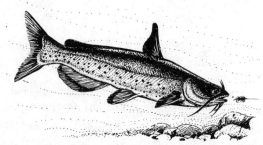

Channel Catfish

CATFISH (Catfish Family). Principally warm- and cool-water scavenger fish, catfish are abundant in most sluggish streams and lakes. They feed mainly by smell and touch at night or in murky waters and by sight in some situations. They can be caught on flies that imitate their favorite natural foods, such as minnows, crayfish, aquatic worms, larger aquatic insects, and terrestrial plant seeds and fruits. The channel and bullhead catfish are most easily caught on scented, slow, deep-fished flies during the day or on the surface at night. They average from one to three pounds, but several species will grow to twenty or even fifty pounds. Despite their looks, they are considered one of the best freshwater fish for the table.

GAR (Gar Family). An armor-plated cool- and warm-water prehistoric fish with fiercely toothed jaws that would shame a pike or alligator, the gar is abundant in most lakes and streams of the Mississippi and Ohio river systems as well as all the Southern states west to Texas. All three major species, short-nosed, long-nosed, and alligator gar, are aggressive minnow predators and will strike most flies that imitate them. Because of their excessive rows of teeth, in iron-hard jaws, they are best caught on nylon-floss hookless streamers. Gar are fun to catch, but take extreme care not to touch their mouths or you will surely be cut or bitten.

This rundown of fish that are favored by fly fishers is a list of only some of the popular and abundant fish that will strike flies. There are several dozen more freshwater species and at least 100 saltwater species (such as tarpon, bonefish, bluefish, snapper, stripers, billfish, shark, and mullet). A lot of the adventure, fun, and excitement of fly-fishing is in catching traditional as well as unconventional fly-rod fish. To learn more about these fish and how to identify them, refer to A. J. McClane's *Field Guide to Freshwater Fishes of North America* and its companion book *Guide to Saltwater Fishes of North America*.

7

Tying Flies

Fly-tying, the hand manufacture of fish-food imitations for fly-fishing, is a major facet of the sport. Anyone who can fly-fish can and should learn to tie flies.

Tying flies is an utterly fascinating and relaxing pastime that may very well double your pleasure and success at the sport of fly-fishing. It is a perfect off- and in-season indoor complement to fly-fishing. Imitating natural fish foods or creating attracter flies and catching fish on your own handmade flies is a unique pleasure, and it gives a great sense of pride. There is no limit to fish foods you can imitate by tying flies.

Fly-tying is merely wrapping a thread around a hook, binding to the hook various tying materials (hair, feathers, yarns, or tinsels) to simulate a fish food. With a basic set of simple tools, tying materials, and a few tying instructions, you can learn how to tie flies in a few hours. You will be amazed at how well fish will strike your own hand-tied flies.

Getting started fly-tying is not expensive if you keep your involvement simple and basic, gradually expanding as your interest, skill, and finances allow. Since the cost of most commercial flies reflects the hand labor more than materials, tying your own may cost you only a few cents each. Almost without exception, amateur fly tiers produce more flies than they can use, so their excess make wonderful gifts or create extra income to cover the expense of the sport.

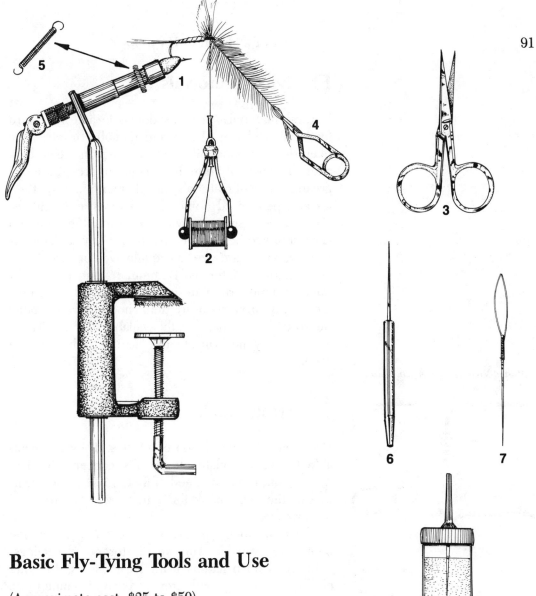

Basic Fly-Tying Tools and Use

(Approximate cost: $25 to $50)

1. Vise—Holds hook during tying.
2. Bobbin—Holds thread during tying.
3. Needle-point scissors—Cuts and trims tying materials.
4. Hackle pliers—Holds small or delicate feathers.
5. Vise material clip—Fits on vise cam and holds materials ready for use.
6. Bodkin and half-hitch tool—Bodkin point picks and separates materials. Half-hitch tool helps form half-hitch knot.
7. Simple nylon-loop whip-finish tool—Helps form whip-finish knot.
8. Head cement—Glues, coats, and adds finish.

Fly-Tying Materials

Natural materials, such as domestic and wild bird feathers, wild animal hair and metallic tinsels, have been the traditional pillars of fly-tying. In recent decades, however, fly tiers have come to accept a much greater range of materials, mostly man-made synthetics and pen-raised domesticated birds and animals. There is evergrowing evidence that either modern natural or synthetic materials, if properly selected for texture, color, and size, do equally well or excel traditional natural materials. Remember that most traditional and modern fly designs and their color patterns are simply products of fly tiers choosing from among the suitable materials locally available to them. There is practically no limit to the materials that can be used.

Mustad-Viking #7958 in actual sizes.

Fly-Tying Hooks

Hooks are the foundation of all flies. They are available to accommodate almost any conceivable size, design, and imitation need of fly tiers. It is important to use the right hook for a fly's size, density, and performance.

The tying tools, materials, hooks, and instruction books are available from retail stores and catalogs. Seek tying instructions from local clinics, fly-tying clubs, or sporting-goods stores. As you become more familiar with the tools and materials of fly-tying, you will most likely enjoy making certain tools and gathering materials from hunting trips or excursions to taxidermists or other materials stores. Discovering a new tool or material is a bonus adventure to the sport.

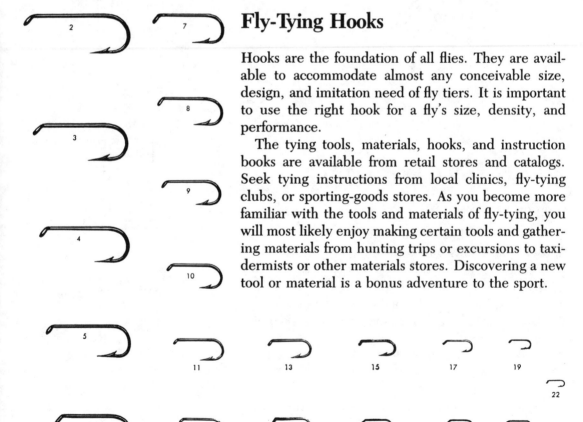

Hook Parts

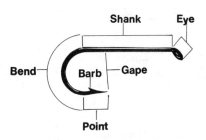

The Parts of a Hook

Eye. The looped opening at the end of the hook that allows attachment of the leader's tip or tippet to the fly. Types of hook eyes include the ringed eye (R), turned-up eye (TU), turned-down eye (TD), ball-eye (B), and looped eye (L).

Shank. The hook's section that provides the length and foundation for attaching or tying the materials to it. Shank lengths include extra short (XS) and extra long (XL).

Bend. The curved portion that forms the hook size and shape. Bend types describe hook shape: round, limerick, sproat, and so on.

Point. The sharp or spear-shaped lower end portion that penetrates the fish's mouth.

Barb. Just behind the point, the barb aids in keeping the hook lodged in the mouth tissue of the fish.

Gap. The distance between the point and the shank. This distance determines the hook's size.

Tying a Woolly Worm Wet Fly

Woolly Worm

The Woolly Worm wet fly is a simple fly to tie, yet it involves most of the basic fly-tying procedures. It is also a very effective fly design for taking all types of fish. Listed below are the materials you will need to create your own Wooly Worm:

HOOK: Mustad 9671, TDE 2XL, Size #6.
THREAD: Waxed monocord, black.
TAIL: Tip of hackle (rooster feather).
BODY: Medium black chenille.
BODY HACKLE: three to four-inch long neck or saddle hackle.
CEMENT: Clear head cement.

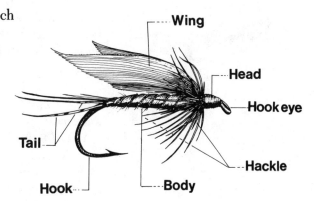

General artificial-fly parts

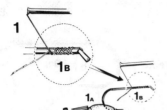

TYING PROCEDURE. *Step 1A.* Position hook in vise jaws so that the point and barb are not covered by vise jaws and the shank is almost parallel to table top. Tighten jaws just enough to grip hook firmly.

Step 1B. Pull out about three inches of thread from bobbin. Hold it tight against middle shank with left hand; hold bobbin in right hand. Now wrap thread firmly with the bobbin over, down, under, and back over hook (clockwise) shank, working toward hook eye. Stop just short of eye, and wrap back over first wraps. This process locks thread on hook shank. Now wrap thread back to hook bend and trim excess thread tip away with scissors. Thread-wrapped hook shank provides a better surface to attach and cement materials.

Step 2A. Tail. With your scissors, cut the tip off the end of the hackle feather for the fly's tail. It should be one-third as long as the hook shank.

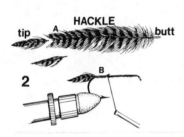

Step 2B. With your left thumb and index finger, hold the hackle tip just over the junction of the hook shank and bend. With your thread bobbin, make about two or three loose wraps around the hook and the feather stem while still holding the feather tip. Now tighten those wraps and make about six more over the hook and feather stem.

In most cases of attaching materials to the hook shank with thread, making several loose wraps before tightening (rather than tightening each wrap as you go) is a much easier method of ensuring that the material will remain in position when thread is tightened.

Release your hold on the feather, and check its position. If it seems a bit out of line, simply pull or twist it into position.

Step 3. Attachment of hackle. Just at the end of the hook shank, next to the tail, place the hackle end with your left thumb and index finger. Wrap thread closely around it three or four times, and then tighten wraps. Now make about six more tight wraps over the tied-down hackle end to secure it. Place hackle butt in material clip.

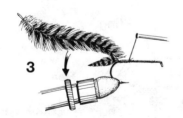

Step 4A. Body chenille attachment. Cut a strand of chenille about four or five times the length of the hook shank. On one end, pull away some of the fuzzy fibers to expose about one-eighth inch or more of the chenille's thread core.

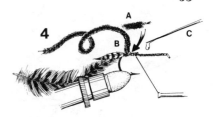

Step 4B. Now place this thread tip just beside the tail and hackle tie-down area (at the shank and bend junction) and wrap it down.

Step 4C. Body cementing. Lightly overcoat the entire hook shank with head cement. This glues the attached materials and seals the hook shank and thread wraps against becoming wet. It also provides a modest adhesion to the body material that is next to be wrapped over the shank.

Step 5A. Body. Advance thread to just behind the hook eye.

Step 5B. Wrap the chenille around the hook shank. Begin at the hook's bend. Wrap the chenille in the same direction as the thread is wrapped. Space wraps so that they just touch each other.

Step 5C. Stop wrapping just before you get to the hook eye—about one wrap away. With thread, cross-wrap the chenille to tie it down to the hook shank. Make about six to eight firm thread wraps, and clip away excess chenille.

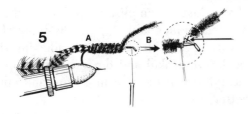

Step 6. Body hackle. Grasp the hackle butt with your right hand and wrap the feather around the body to the hook eye. Make a forward spiral wrap, about as many turns as you made with the chenille.

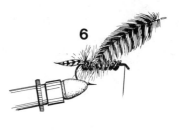

Step 7. When the hackle has been wrapped to behind the hook eye, make one full wrap and then tie down the stem with your thread. Trim away the excess stem and butt.

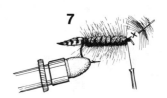

Do not crowd the hook eye with the hackle wrap or there will not be enough space to make the fly head and finish. Study the illustrations very closely to avoid this and other possible problems.

Step 8A. With tying thread, wrap over the chenille and hackle tie-down area to cover them and to form a neat, small, thread head. Head wraps should be just up to hook eye but not over it. Make sure wraps are smoothly placed and tight.

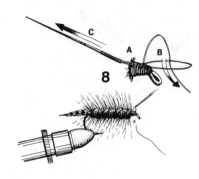

Step 8B. Head whip finish. Place the nylon loop whip-finish tool with loop over fly's head. Make about 6 to 10 firm (but not tight) wraps over the loop and head, advancing from back of head toward hook eye and loop end.

Step 8C. Pull about six inches of thread off bobbin spool. While holding the thread tight with your left-hand fingers, cut the thread so it is about three or four inches long. Now place thread end through nylon loop. Keep tension on thread so wraps will not loosen or unwind.

Step 8D. Grasp whip-finisher handle and pull back so that loop slides under wraps until it pulls free, pulling thread end with it. Next tighten thread wraps of whip finish by pulling on thread end. Trim away excess thread with scissors as close as possible to head.

Step 9. Head finish. Paint the thread wraps carefully with one or two coats of head cement. Take care not to plug fly's eye with cement or allow any to get on body or hackle.

You have just accomplished many of the most important techniques and steps in fly-tying. Repeat tying this fly several times at least, allowing time to relax and let your skill and dexterity develop. Each time, the tying will become more fun and you'll do much better, too.

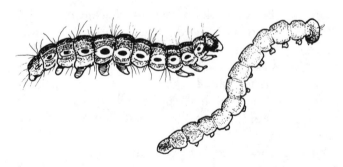

8

Fly-Fishing Safety

The most common accidents experienced while fly-fishing are falling, hooking yourself or another person, and being bitten or cut on hands or fingers by a fish. All of these accidents are easily avoided or made less likely when you take a few basic precautions.

Avoid Falling

Most falls while you are fly-fishing occur while wading fast-flowing, irregular-bottom streams. Loss of balance happens most frequently when you are in water that's from an inch deep to, or just above, your knees. In such shallow water, you have much confidence, and you tend to step or walk quickly and without caution. In deeper water you step more slowly and cautiously, and the deeper water helps hold you erect.

To avoid falls, be sure to wear a wading boot or shoe that has a sole and heel made to grip the type of bottom you're on. Rubber-cleat soles are best for sand, fine gravel, soft silt, or mud. Felt soles are best for bottoms made up of irregular-size rocks and flat bedrock covered by slick algae. The felt actually scrubs the algae away and grips the rough rock surface. Take great care in walking up or down wet dirt, clay, or leaf-laden banks while wearing felt-soled shoes. These surfaces may be as slippery as ice.

In swift water over hard, slick rock bottoms, use soles that have felt or soft-metal stud or cleat combinations. The metal actually cuts and sticks on the rock's surface. But take care with this combination while walking over dry rocks, as you lose some traction.

No sole material can compensate for careless foot-work. Learn to shuffle and feel your footing from step to step. Do not pick up one foot until the other is firmly in place. Whenever possible, watch for bottom pitfalls through Polaroid sunglasses. Large boulders, flat, slick rocks, depressions, tree limbs, loose rocks, and drop offs can put you down quickly if you do not see, feel, or suspect them.

You will have an easier time wading if you use a wading staff as your searching "foot" or foundation as you take each step. You can select a stout streamside stick or buy a special wading staff. The Folstaff folds conveniently when not in use and immediately unfolds when you need it for wading or hiking to or from the stream.

Wade Carefully!

Try not to wade against the current. Wherever possible, cross by going with the current. If you lose your footing or balance, you can slap your fly rod down on the water to regain balance without harming the fly rod. If you do fall or wade over your head, do not fight the current. Relax and go with it. Keep your feet downstream and your head upstream until the water or a friend helps you to safety. If you are fly-fishing with a companion, help each other wade safely across bad stretches. One way is to place your hand on his shoulder. Another way is to hold hands. Four legs are twice as safe as two—any dog, cat, or horse can tell you that!

Never wade in above your knees while wearing hip-high waders. Do not wear such waders in a boat or where you might fall into water over your head. They quickly fill and affect your ability to swim.

When wearing chest-high waders, *always* wear a belt around the outside of them to prevent them from filling if you wade too deep or fall. It is a good idea to experiment by going too deep in waders or hippers in a swimming pool, with a friend standing by, just to get a sense of what happens should you fall down or go too deep while fishing. The experience may well save your life or another's life. Your clothing and waders will hold air and remain buoyant to a certain extent. This will keep you floating if you do not struggle or swim violently.

Fish Bites

Fish bites, cuts, or punctures are very common hand injuries. What causes them are a fish's sharp teeth, sharp gill-plate edges, and spined fins. Some of these wounds are very painful, and occasionally infectious and even poisonous. So it pays to use certain precautions when landing and handling any fish. A dip net, a tailer, a gaff, and various mouth-opening and hook-removal tools will, if used properly, almost entirely eliminate these dangers.

First, do not get so excited when you land or un-hook a fish that you forget to keep your hands and fingers away from its mouth, gill plates, and fins. Learn which fish can hurt, and how. For instance, all trout, char, and salmon have sharp teeth, but none have cutting gill plates or sharp, spined fins. A snook has a harmless mouth but razor-sharp gill plates and needle-sharp dorsal-fin spines.

So keep the fish out of your hands by using a net or by beaching it. Keep your fingers out of its mouth or off gill plates by using a hemostat or needle-nose pliers or hook disgorger to unhook it.

Hooking Accidents

When you practice fly-casting on the lawn or over water, use a hookless practice fly or cut the hook off an ordinary fly. Wear a hat, glasses, long-sleeved shirt, and long trousers for protection. Such apparel almost completely protects you from the most common hooking accidents.

Watch where you and everyone else is located, and do not get in each other's casting paths. On windy days, be particularly careful about where your fly goes on the backcast. Never try to jerk a hooked fly loose from hangups on backward or forward casts without taking care that it will not snap back and hit you.

When you wade, keep a good distance away from other anglers and watch the wind's effect on the fly. In a boat, be very careful of the other occupants, and try to keep the boat angled so you do not allow your backcast to travel over the boat. If you are right-handed and you cast from the bow to the shoreline, keep the boat moving parallel to the left shoreline. Then your backcast will be ahead of the boat. The opposite is best for the left-handed bow caster.

If you should hook yourself or someone else, there are several actions you might take for safe hook removal. First, if it is a barbless hook, just grasp the fly and remove it by reversing the entry path. If the hook has a barb and it has penetrated past the barb, the situation may be a bit more serious. First, do not panic. After all, the hook has done very little tissue damage, so just relax. Ninety-nine percent of all hooks can be painlessly and quickly removed.

If someone is with you, let him remove it; if you are alone, you can do so if the hook is easily reached by both hands. If not, cut the leader tip off the fly, and seek help elsewhere.

Should the fly be lodged in your eye socket area, or buried in the skull bones or in the throat or neck, *go immediately to the emergency room of the nearest hospital!*

Here are steps to follow when the situation is one in which you decide that you or a companion should remove the hook: (1) Cut off the leader at or near the fly, and put your fly rod aside. (2) Determine if hook is just buried or has turned and exited out your skin. Most hooks will be buried. If it is just buried past the bend, follow procedure A. Follow procedure B if it is turned back out.

Procedure A (for a hook just buried past the bend). Take a section of heavy nylon monofilament, or other fishing line or fly-line, long enough to secure a firm handhold on it when it is doubled. Pass it through the hook bend and back toward the direction opposite where the hook entered. With one hand, take a firm grip on the doubled section of line, just a few inches from the hook bend. With the other hand, press down the hook eye (fly-head area) with your index finger or thumb against the skin. While pressing down on the

How to Remove Hook That Has Penetrated Into Skin Beyond Barb

1. Cut leader

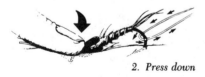

2. Press down

3. Press down and pull

hook eye, make a straight smooth, quick, firm, pull on the doubled line away from the direction the hook entered. The fly will pop immediately out without pain or tissue damage. Some bleeding may occur, but that is okay as it will help flush the wound. Encourage the bleeding awhile, then stop it by applying direct pressure.

Procedure B (for a hook that is turned back out). This removal method can only be attempted if you have a pair of side-cutting diagonals (dikes) or pliers. If you do not, do not attempt removal but go to an emergency room of a hospital or to a physician for assistance. Check the hook to see that the barb has cleared the skin. If it has not, push it on out. Cut off the point and barb with side-cutting pliers and remove the de-barbed hook by backing it out along the same path by which it entered.

In either case, treat the wound with antiseptic and cover it temporarily with a sterile bandage. As soon as convenient, consult a physician about the need for a tetanus shot.

How to Remove Hook Whose Point Has Penetrated Skin and Then Emerged

1. Cut leader

2. Cut off point and barb

3. Back out

9
The Years Ahead

Once you've learned the basics of fly-fishing, you're ready to reap the rewards. You'll find that fly-fishing will greatly multiply your pleasure on the water; you'll enjoy the process of casting itself, and you'll enjoy the special thrill of tempting a really difficult fish to your fly—perhaps one you've tied yourself.

It won't all be easy. You can't learn all of fly-fishing in a week or from any book. Skill takes motivation and practice. You'll have to be patient with your flaws and try steadily to correct them. There will be frustrations—wind knots, sloppy casts, the inability to match a specific hatch of insects when fish are rising to them everywhere in sight, times when you're fly tying and you seem to have nine thumbs. You must *want* to perfect your techniques and you must practice constantly. Believe me, it's worth the effort.

For fly-fishing can provide a lifetime of pleasure—and part of that pleasure lies in improving your skills, becoming more adept at the various arts of fly-fishing, gaining more and more experience on the water.

Of course the future of *your* fly-fishing depends in part upon the future of everyone's fly-fishing—and that depends upon the protection of our quarry and of the waters in which they live. More and more people are coming to love the *quality* of their fishing. They want to fish for wild fish in clean, natural surroundings. Fewer people are killing their fish today. They realize that tempting a fish to the fly and playing it on balanced fly tackle is not only the best part of fishing but also that it provides fish to tempt another day. Sections of many rivers are now under "catch and release" restrictions and the quality of the fishing they provide has improved immensely.

Because a lot of serious fishermen have worked hard to protect our waters, the future of fly-fishing is bright today. But you'll have to help if it's to remain so. Keep improving your skills; keep trying to catch more and more species of fish on the fly; help protect our fisheries—and have lots of fun fly-fishing!

Appendices

Fly Assortments

STANDARD DRY-FLY SELECTION FOR TROUT
Adams, #14, #16, #18
Light Cahill, #12, #16, #18
Quill Gordon, #12, #14, #16
Black Gnat, #14, #16, #18
Blue Wing Olive, #14, #16, #18
Hendrickson, #10, #12, #14
March Brown, #10, #12, #14

SPECIAL DRY FLIES
Gray Fox Variant, #12, #14
Brown Spider, #10, #12
Dun Variant, #14, #16
Brown Bivisible, #10, #12
Adams Parachute, #12, #14, #16
Irresistible, #12, #14, #16
Royal Wulff, #10, #14
Henryville Caddis, #12, #14, #16

DRY-FLY TERRESTRIALS
Black Ant, #12, #14, #16
Cinnamon Ant, #14, #16, #18
Beetle (black), #10, #14, #18
Dave's Hopper, #8, #10, #12
Jassid, #16, #18, #20
Green Inchworm, #10, #12, #14
Cricket (black), #10, #12, #14

MATCH-THE-HATCH DRY-FLY SERIES
No-hackles or Compara-duns
Dun, gray wing, yellow body, #16, #18, #20
   slate-gray wing, olive body, #14, #16, #18, #20
   slate-gray wing, tan body, #12, #14, #18, #20
No-hackle Hen or Poly Spinners
   white wing, black body, #18, #20, #22
   light gray wing, yellow body, #16, #18, #20
   light gray wing, reddish-brown body, #14, #16, #18
   light gray wing, gray-olive body, #12, #14, #16
Paraduns
   dun-gray wing, tan body, #8, #10, #12
   slate-gray wing, olive body, #8, #10, #12
   cream wing, yellow body, #6, #8, #10

Elk Hair Caddis or Borger Poly Caddis
   tan wing, brown body, #12, #14, #16, #18
   tan wing, olive body, #14, #16, #18
   tan wing, gray body, #12, #14, #16
   tan wing, orange body, #6, #8, #10

STANDARD WET FLIES
Leadwing Coachman, #10, #12, #14
Royal Coachman, #10, #12, #14
Light Cahill, #12, #14
Parmachene Belle, #8, #10, #12
Black Gnat, #12, #14, #16
Iron Blue Dun, #12, #14, #16
Gray Hackle Yellow, #10, #12, #14
Gray Hackle Peacock, #10, #12, #14
Black and Grizzly Woolly Worm, #6, #8, #10

NYMPHS
Gold-Ribbed Hare's Ear, #10, #12, #14, #16
Tellico, #10, #12
Zug Bug, #10, #12, #14
Darkstone, #2, #4, #6
Brownstone, #4, #6, #8
Goldenstone, #6, #8, #10
Dave's Shrimp, #12, #14, #16
Gray Nymph, #8, #10, #12
Red Squirrel Nymph, #8, #10, #12, #14
Damsel Nymph, #8, #10

STANDARD STREAMER ASSORTMENT
Gray Ghost, #2, #6, #10
Black-nose Dace, #4, #6, #8
Mickey Finn, #6, #8, #10
Muddler Minnow, #2, #6, #10
Black Ghost, #4, #6, #8
White Marabou, #4, #6, #8
Black Marabou, #2, #4, #6
Yellow Marabou, #6, #8, #10
Dark Spruce (golden), #2, #4, #6, #8
Light Spruce (silver), #4, #6, #8, #10
Hornberg, #2, #4

SALMON FLIES (WET)
Silver Gray, #2, #6, #8
Blue Charm, #2, #6, #8, #10
Rusty Rat, #4, #5, #8, #10
Black Dose, #4, #6, #8, #10

Cosseboom, #2, #4, #6, #8
Jock Scott, #2, #4, #6
Muddler, #2, #4, #6, #8
Butterfly, #4, #6, #8

SALMON FLIES (DRY)

Bomber, #1/0, #4, #8
White Wulff, #4, #5, #12
Rat-Faced McDougal, #4, #6, #8
Royal Wulff, #4, #6, #8
Mackintosh, #2, #4, #6
Salmon Skater, #8
Dave's Adult Stonefly, #2, #4, #6

BASS AND PIKE BUG ASSORTMENT (TOPWATER)

Most Whit Hair Bug (yellow, black, red and
white), #2, #6, #10
Near Nuff Hair Frog, #2, #6, #10
Marabou Moth Bug (black, brown, yellow), #2,
#6, #10
Hula Popper (yellow, frog, black), #1/0, #4
Pencil Popper (yellow, white, black), #1/0, #4
Slider Bug (yellow, black, white), #1/0, #4

Muddler Minnow (natural, black, white, yellow), #1/0, #4, #8
Dalberg Diver Bug (frog, yellow, black, grizzly,
silver minnow, and perch), #2, #6, #10

BASS AND PIKE FLIES (UNDERWATER)

Eelworm streamer (black, yellow, white), #1/0,
#4
Grass Shrimp (gray, pink, tan, gold), #1/0, #4,
#8, #10
Glass Minnow (white, blue and white, brown
and white), #1/0, #4, #6, #8
Sea Ducer (red and yellow, red and white),
#2/0, #4
Lefty's Deceiver (white, yellow, roach, red and
white, black, blue and white), #2/0, #2, #6
Tarpon Special (yellow grizzly, blue grizzly,
cockroach, orange grizzly), #3/0, #1/0
Skipping Popper (red and white, yellow, blue
and white), #3/0, #1/0
Pencil Popper (yellow, white, silver, black),
#3/0, #1/0, #4
Muddler Minnow, #3/0, #1/0, #4, #8

Books and Periodicals for Fly Fishermen

BOOKS ON FLY-TYING

Most Important

Art Flick's Master Fly Tying Guide by Art Flick et al.
Flies (new edition) by J. Edson Leonard
Fly Tying Materials by Eric Leiser
Universal Fly Tying Guide by Dick Stewart (excellent for beginners)

Excellent

American Nymph Fly Tying Manual by Randall Kaufmann
The Fly Tyer's Almanac by Robert Boyle and Dave Whitlock
Popular Fly Patterns by Terry Hellekson
Saltwater Flies by Kenneth Bay
The Second Fly Tyer's Almanac by Robert Boyle and Dave Whitlock
Tying the Swisher and Richards Flies by Doug Swisher and Carl Richards

Good

Atlantic Salmon Flies and Fishing by Joseph D. Bates, Jr.
The Complete Book of Fly Tying by Eric Leiser
Dick Surette's Fly Index by Dick Surette
Fly Tying and Fly Fishing for Bass and Panfish by Tom Nixon
Modern Dressing for the Practical Angler by Poul Jorgensen
Salmon Flies by Poul Jorgensen
Streamers and Bucktails by Joseph D. Bates, Jr.
Tying and Fishing the Fuzzy Nymphs by Polly Rosborough
Tying and Fishing Terrestrials by Gerald Almy
Western Trout Fly Tying Manual by Jack Dennis

BOOKS ON FLY-FISHING

Most Important
Dave Whitlock's Guide to Aquatic Trout Foods by Dave Whitlock
Fly Fishing in Salt Water by Lefty Kreh
Masters on the Dry Fly, edited by J. Migel
Masters on the Nymph, edited by J. Migel and Leonard Wright
Selective Trout by Doug Swisher and Carl Richards

Excellent
Art Flick's New Streamside Guide to Naturals and Their Imitations by
   Art Flick
The Caddis and the Angler by Larry Solomon and Eric Leiser
Fishing the Dry Fly as a Living Insect by Leonard Wright
Fly Casting with Lefty Kreh by Lefty Kreh
Fly Fishing for Trout by Dick Talleur
Fly Fishing Strategy by Doug Swisher and Carl Richards
Lamar Underwood's Bass Almanac
Naturals by Gary Borger
Steelhead Fly Fishing and Flies by Trey Combs
Through the Fish's Eyes by Mark Sosin and John Clark
Trout by Ray Bergman
Trout Fishing by Joe Brooks

PERIODICALS

Angler Magazine, Box 12155, Oakland, CA 94604
   Regular features on Western saltwater fly-fishing and fly-tying.

The Flyfisher, P.O. Box 1088, West Yellowstone, MT 59758
   The official magazine of the Federation of Fly Fishers (FFF), published
   quarterly. Membership to FFF includes subscription to the magazine.

Flyfishing, P.O. Box 02112, Portland, OR 97202
   Features fly-fishing and fly-tying.

Fly Fisherman, Box 8200, Harrisburg, PA 17105
   Feature articles on fly-fishing and fly-tying throughout the world.

Fly Tyer, Box 1231, North Conway, NH 03860
   Quarterly on fly-tying.

International Flyfisher, 39 Mayfield Road, Belvedere, Kent, England
   Magazine presenting interesting articles on flies.

Rod and Reel, Box 1309, Manchester Center, VT 05255
   Interesting fly-fishing articles.

The Roundtable, United Fly Tyers, Inc., P.O. Box 723, Boston, MA 02102
   Membership in United Fly Tyers, a nonprofit international organization,
   includes subscription. Articles on fly-tying with how-to instruction.

Salmon Trout Steelheader, P.O. Box 02112, Portland, OR 97202
   Often describes how to tie best Western patterns.

Scientific Angler's Handbooks, Scientific Anglers, P.O. Box 2001, Midland,
  MI 48640
  Annual handbooks on general fly-fishing, bass fly-fishing, panfish fly-
  fishing, and saltwater fly-fishing.

Trout, P.O. Box 1944, Washington, D.C. 20013
  The official magazine of Trout Unlimited (TU), published quarterly.
  TU membership includes subscription.

Major Fly-Fishing Organizations

FEDERATION OF FLY FISHERMEN, P.O. Box 1088, West
Yellowstone, MT 59758.
The federation has over 200 clubs nationally, conducting all types of fly-
fishing, fly-tying, and conservation activities. With membership you receive
an excellent news bulletin and *the flyfisher* magazine.

TROUT UNLIMITED, P.O. Box 1944, Washington, D.C. 20013.
Trout Unlimited has chapters throughout the United States and Canada. It
has trout and salmon-fishing and conservation activities. Local chapters
active in fly-fishing and fly-tying seminars. With membership you receive a
news bulletin and *Trout* magazine.

UNITED FLY TYERS, INC., P.O. Box 723, Boston, MA 02102.
Active in all types of fly-tying and fly-fishing promotion and instruction. Has
excellent magazine, the *Roundtable*, on fly-tying.

SALTWATER FLY RODDERS OF AMERICA, P.O. Box 304,
Cape May Court House, NJ 08120.
Active in all types of saltwater fly-fishing and fly-tying. Also has magazine
with membership.

Glossary

Action—A word that expresses the flexibility and power of a fly rod.

AFTMA—American Fishing Tackle Manufacturers Association. American fishing-tackle manufacturers organized to maintain standards of fishing tackle, public information, product quality, marketing, and conservation of the resource.

Arbor—The spindle of a fly-reel spool that the backing line is attached to and wound on.

Aquatic insects—Those insects that live some part of their normal life cycle beneath the water.

Attracter (color)—Unnaturally bright color in a fly pattern.

Backing (braided)—A line most commonly composed of several filaments of either nylon or Dacron braided into a single component. Used to extend fly line's length.

Bank—The higher and steeper sides above a lake or stream, usually created by water cutting or eroding the shoreline.

Bar—A mounded structure in streams and some lakes caused by accumulation of rock, sand, sediment, and dead vegetation, usually protruding out of the water or very near the surface.

Barb (hook)—The raised cut section of a hook immediately behind the point. It prevents hook from coming out of the fish's mouth.

Barbless hook—A fly hook without a barb.

Bass—A general descriptive term for a group of larger freshwater sunfish, particularly largemouth bass, smallmouth bass, and Kentucky or spotted bass.

Bassbug—A floating fly used for bass fly-fishing.

Beaching—A method of landing a fish by coaxing or forcing it to swim or drift itself aground in the shallow water of a lake or stream shoreline.

Beaver pond—A small lake, usually less than two acres, which has been formed by the damming of small brook or stream by beavers.

Belly—The larger midsection of a fly line. Also may refer to the curve of a fly-line midsection when wind or current pushes it into a C shape.

Bite—A term often used by fly fishers to describe the strike of a fish. Bite also may refer to the distance from hook point and the extent of the bend.

Brackish water—Water that has less salt content than true ocean salt water. Occurs most commonly where freshwater streams meet or mix with saltwater bays and estuaries.

Breakoff—The accidental or purposeful breaking of the leader tippet from a hooked fish—freeing it.

Bucktail—A streamer fly constructed from the hair of a deer's tail (bucktail).

Bug—Usually refers to a floating bass fly that might imitate various large insects, frogs, mice, and so on.

Buttcap—The end of a fly-rod handle used for resting and protecting the fly rod and fly reel when stored upright. At times it is rested against the fly fisher's stomach when fighting a large fish.

Canal—A manmade, water-filled ditch used to join lakes or swamps to rivers, or to straighten and quicken the flow of a stream's runoff.

Cast—The act of delivering the fly to the fishing area with fly-rod line and leader. Cast is also used as a descriptive term by the English fly fisher to denote the fly leader.

Catch and release—An expression for catching fish, with immediate release alive and unharmed.

Channel—The main depression caused by flowing water (current).

Char—A group of popular freshwater fish that includes brook trout, lake trout, arctic char, and Dolly Varden.

Chenille—A fly-tying popular material consisting of fine fibers of rayon, wool, nylon, and so on that are bound together in a uniform cord with two or more twisted threads. Especially popular on underwater flies such as the Woolly Worm.

Chumline—A series of fish food pieces put into the water to attract and congregate hungry fish in a specific area near the fisherman.

Clippers—A small tool used to cut and trim the fly line, leader, or tippet material.

Cold-water fish—Fish that thrive best in water temperature ranges from 40° to 60°. For example: trout, char, grayling, and salmon.

Cool-water fish—Fish that thrive best in water temperature ranges from 55° to 70°. For example: smallmouth bass, shad, walleyes, Northern pike, whitefish, striped bass.

Corkers—Rubber sandals with sharp hard-metal cleats in their soles that are worn over waders, boots, or shoes to increase grip or traction on very slippery rock stream bottoms.

Cork rings—Rings of cork that are glued together and shaped to form the fly-rod handle.

Cove—A small water indentation in the shoreline of a lake or ocean.

Crayfish—A freshwater lobsterlike small crustacean very popular as fish food.

Creel—A container cooled by water evaporation used to keep and carry dead fish.

Crossbar (fly reel)—A part of a fly-reel frame that is chiefly for structural support between the two sides. Sometimes referred to as a post.

Cruising (fish)—An expression describing a fish that is moving about in lake or stream in order to find food.

Crustacea—An important group of fresh- and salt-water aquatic invertebrates which are fed upon by many fish. Shrimp, scud, sowbugs, crabs, and crayfish are examples.

Current—The flowing or gravitational pull of water in a stream. Lakes and oceans also have currents.

Deaddrift—The drift of a fly downstream without action other than what is given it by the natural current flow. It means no drag.

Deer hair—Body hair, usually coarse and semi-hollow, from various deer. Used for tying many fly designs and patterns.

Density—Refers to the weight of fly line, leader, or fly compared to the weight of the water. *High density* means much heavier than water and fast sinking. *Low density* means slow sinking or even floating.

Dipnet—The device used to scoop up and hold a hooked fish. Also called a landing net.

Double hook—A fly-hook design that has two points, barbs, and bends, and one common shank. Most commonly used for making Atlantic salmon flies.

Drag (guides)—The rod's guides and fly line create points of friction that are often referred to as drag.

Drag (line)—An expressive term used to describe a current or wind pull on the fly line that results in pulling the fly unnaturally over or through the water.

Drag (reel)—A part of the fly reel that adjusts the spool's tension when line is pulled off the reel by the fly fisher or a fish.

Dress—The application of waterproofing or flotant material to the fly line, leader, or fly.

Drift—Describes the path a fly travels while it is fished down the stream's current.

Dry fly—A basic fly design that floats on the water's surface. It is usually made of low density, waterproof materials to hold in the water's surface film.

Dry-fly paste—A paste compound used to waterproof the water-absorbent materials of floating flies.

Dry-fly spray—Aerosol spray compound used to waterproof the water-absorbent materials of a dry fly.

Dubbing—A fly-tying material consisting of natural hairs and/or synthetic fibers blended into a loose felt and used to form the body of many floating and sinking flies.

Dun—The term used to identify the first adult stage (subimago) of mayfly aquatic insects. Also a descriptive term generally referring to a gray or dull color common on mayfly duns.

Eddy—A calm, slowly swirling (upstream) water flow in a stream behind an obstruction such as a boulder, log, bar, or moss bed.

Emerger—A term to identify the stage of natural or fly imitation of an aquatic insect as it swims to the surface to hatch or transform from nymph or pupa to adult.

Feeding—A fish's eating or striking period.

Fighting—The act of tiring a hooked fish in preparation of landing it.

Fingerling—A general descriptive term used to describe various larger fish species (trout, bass, catfish, etc.) when they are about finger-length in size.

Fishery—A body of water that sustains a healthy fish population and has potential for fly-fishing success.

Fish for fun—Catching and immediately releasing fish alive and unharmed. Usually it is illegal to keep or kill fish caught in these designated areas.

Fishing vest—A vest with assorted pockets for carrying the various flies, reels, and accessories used while walking, wading, or fly-fishing.

Flat—A wide shallow-water section of a lake, stream, or ocean. Flats usually have a relatively uniform smooth surface.

Flotant—Material used to waterproof fly lines, leaders, and flies.

Fly—The artificial lure used in fly-fishing.

Fly design—Describes type of fly or purpose of fly.

Fly pattern—The color and material makeup of a particular fly design.

Fly tier—A person who makes or "ties" flies for fly-fishing.

Freestone stream—A stream that has a relatively high bottom gradient made up mostly of coarse gravel or rubble and whose source of water is mainly runoff rain and melting snow.

Freshwater—Water with little or no salt content. It also refers to fish species that are adapted only to freshwater environs.

Fry—The first stage of development of a fish after hatching from the egg or live birth. Usually from one-half to two inches in length.

Gaff—A hook-and-handle tool used to hook and capture larger fish. Also refers to the act of hooking and capturing a fish once it has been tired with rod and reel.

Gamefish—A general term used to denote those species of fish that will readily strike or attack an artificial lure or fly. Also deals with the ability and willingness of the fish to fight very hard after it is hooked.

Gap—The distance between the hook shank and the point.

Gill—The respiratory organ of a water-breathing fish, located just behind the head.

Giving butt—Using the fly-rod butt section to slow or stop a hard-fighting fish's swim.

Giving tip—Holding the rod tip forward and high to provide maximum shock absorption to prevent the leader's tippet from breaking and the fly from being pulled out of the fish's mouth.

Grab—A term often used to describe a brief period fish go through when they are willing to strike a fly.

Grain—The unit of measurement used for calibrating fly-line weights.

Grease—The application of paste to line or fly dressing to enhance flotation.

Hackle—Usually neck and back feathers of a chicken, however, can also be from other chickenlike birds such as grouse or partridge.

Handle (reel)—A crank on a fly-reel spool used for reeling the fly line on to the fly reel.

Handle (rod)—The grip used for holding the fly rod while casting, fishing, and fighting a fish.

Hauling—A method of increasing fly-line speed during pickup, back, or forward casting. It is accomplished by hand pulling on the fly line between the rod's stripper guide and the fly reel.

Hold—A place where a fish such as salmon, trout, or bass will rest or remain stationary for a period of time.

Holding fish—Describes a fish that remains in a particular spot in a lake or stream.

Hook barb—The raised metal slice off the hook's point and bend. The barb helps prevent the hook from backing out of the fish's mouth tissue.

Hook bend—The curved or bent section just behind the hook shank.

Hook eye—The closed loop part of a fly hook to which the leader tip or tippet is attached.

Hook (fly)—The device used to hold a fish that strikes or attempts to eat the fly.

Hook (-ing) **fish**—Setting the hook in a fish's mouth tissue after the fish has struck.

Hookkeeper—The small clip or eyelet at the front of the fly-rod handle used to store the fly when not in use.

Hook point—The needlelike point on the end of the hook's bend. It enhances faster penetration into the fish's mouth tissue.

Hook shank—The length of fly hook exclusive of its eye and bend. Generally it is the section to which the fly materials are tied.

Hook size—The distance or amount of gap on a fly hook or fly. Also refers to the overall length and size of wire the hook is made from. Generally hook sizes range from largest #5/0 to smallest #36.

Immature insect—Refers to insects that have not reached sexual maturity or full growth.

Inlet—The area of a lake, pond, or ocean where a stream flows in.

Jack—A common term usually referring to one- or two-year-old sexually mature male salmon or trout that join older fish in their spawning run.

Jump—When a hooked fish comes up out of the water in an attempt to shake the hook or break the leader.

Knotless—A leader that has no knots tied in it to join different-size sections or tippet.

Land (-ing)—Capturing a hooked fish after it has been tired.

Larva—A term denoting the worm or grublike stage between the egg and pupa of the caddis and midge aquatic insects. Also refers to the common descriptive term of the artificial-fly imitation of the larva.

Leader—The transparent part of the fly-fishing line between the fly line and fly. It may include tippet section.

Leader straightener—A rubber or leather pad used to heat and straighten the coils from a leader.

Leader wallet—A convenient pocketed container for storage of extra leaders to be carried while fly-fishing.

Leech—A bloodsucking, wormlike aquatic invertebrate or a fly imitating it.

Levels—The amount of water or depth of a stream or lake.

Line—Short expression for fly line. When the fly line scares a fish it is commonly referred to as lining it.

Line guard—The part of a fly reel that the fly line passes through or over as it is wound on or off the reel spool. It acts as a guide and reduces wear from line friction.

Loop—The general term describing the *U* shape of the fly line as it unrolls forward or backward during the casting cycle.

Loop to loop—An expression used to describe the joining of fly line to leader, leader to tippet, where a closed loop in each is joined to make the other connection.

Lure—An imitation fish food with one or more hooks on it. As a verb it refers to attracting a fish to strike a fly.

Manipulate—Generally refers to more intricate fly presentation and actions accomplished with fly rods of nine feet or longer.

Mature insect—Insects that have reached sexual maturity or full growth.

Matuka—Generally refers to a special fly design in which feathers are uniquely wrapped to the length of a hook shank and/or body of a fly so that they appear as part of the body. The word *Matuka* originated from a bird, the matukar, whose feathers were popularly used for this type of fly.

Meadow stream—A low-gradient stream that flows in a meandering course mainly through meadows or valleys.

Mending—The act of lifting or rolling the fly line with the rod to reposition it in order to avoid fly drag due to current speeds or wind.

Mesh—The net bag or seine of a dipnet or landing net.

Minnow—A general term used for many species of smaller fishes (one- to eight-inches long), as well as the same sizes of immature larger fish.

Monofilament—A single filament or strand of nylon used for fishing line, leader or tippet materials.

Moss bed—A large underwater growth of aquatic plants.

Mudding—The term used to describe a fish stirring up a visible cloud of mud or silt as it feeds and swims on the bottom.

Muddler—A very popular and effective type of artificial fly that has a large clipped deer-hair head and usually incorporates hair and feathers for its wings.

Neck—A long, narrow body of water usually found at stream's inlet to a lake.

Net—Refers to the act of landing a fish with a dipnet or landing net.

Neutral color—Color and pattern of a fly or natural food that does not contrast with its surroundings.

No-kill—A fishery policy of catching and releasing unharmed live fish.

Nongamefish—A general term used to describe those species of fish that never or seldom strike or attack artificial lures or flies.

Nymph—Refers to the water-breathing or immature stage of aquatic insects. Also a fly that imitates these insects.

Nymphing—Fly-fishing with aquatic nymph imitations. A term used to describe a fish that is foraging for aquatic nymphs.

Outlet—That part of a lake where water flows out.

Palming the reel—The application of a palm against the fly-reel outer spool flange to add extra drag pressure on a fish pulling line off the fly reel.

Panfish—A large group of abundant freshwater gamefish species, generally under two pounds in weight. Included are sunfish, bluegill, yellow perch, white bass, crappie, etc.

Parr—The second stage of development of salmonoids, usually termed fingerlings. Term comes from large dark bands or oval marks on their sides.

Perch—A group of fish including the yellow perch, white perch, darters, and walleyed pike.

Pickup—The lifting of a fly line, leader, and fly off the water as the backcast is begun.

Pike—A group of cold and cool freshwater gamefish including Northern pike, pickerel, and muskie. Sometimes walleyed pike (which is not a true pike but a perch) is included.

Pocket—A depression on the bottom of a stream located in the riffle or run of a stream.

Pocket water—A series of bottom depressions or pockets in a stream riffle or run section.

Point—Refers to the narrow, pointed section of land that juts out into a lake or stream.

Polaroids—A popular term for sunglasses that polarize or filter out certain angles of light rays. They reduce reflective sunlight off water so fish are more easily seen beneath.

Pond—Usually refers to a small lake less than five acres in surface area, except in Maine, where it is often used interchangeably with lake.

Pound test—Refers to the strength of a fishing line, leader, or tippet. Sometimes called breaking strength or test.

Power (casting)—Generally describes the wrist and arm movement used to energize the fly rod during the power stroke to cast the fly line, leader, and fly.

Power (rod)—The degree of efficiency a rod has in casting, hooking, and fishing a fish.

Predator fish—A fish that eats live fish, insects, and other animals.

Presentation—The placement of the fly on or below the water. Also describes the fly's path and action on the water.

Pressure (rod)—How hard a fly fisher pulls, restricts, or fights a hooked fish with the fly rod, reel, and leader determines the amount of pressure being used.

Pumping a fish—Pulling a large fish by using a pumping or rod-butt-lifting action as the fish sounds or pulls away. As the rod is quickly lowered after the pump-up, the reel takes up the line gained on the fish.

Pupa—Generally refers to stage between larva and adult of the caddis and midge aquatic insects. Also common descriptive term used for the artificial fly imitation of the same insects.

Putting down—Fish that have been scared by the fly fisher and stop feeding have been *put down*.

Put and take—A fishery management policy that involves artificial stocking of catchable fish and encouragement of killing and removing these fish when caught.

Rapids—A section of stream that has a high gradient and fast, rough-surfaced flowing water.

Reading water—Visually examining the surface of the water to evaluate fishing potential, depth, and fish location.

Reel—To wind in or retrieve the fly line, leader, backing, etc. Also short expression for fly reel.

Reel hand—The hand and arm used to hold or reel in the fly line. Same as line hand.

Reel saddle—The part of a reel that provides means for attaching the reel to the rod seat and/or handle.

Reel seat—The part of a fly rod, just behind the rod handle, where the fly reel is fastened.

Reel spool—The part of a fly reel where the line is wound and stored.

Riffle—The section of a stream where the water flows shallowly and rapidly over an irregular bottom so that the surface riffles. Also refers to a water surface slightly disturbed by the wind.

Rising fish—A fish that is visibly feeding just below or at the water's surface.

Rod blank—A fly rod before it is fitted with guides and handle or other finished fly-rod accessories.

Rod guides—Also **Fly-rod guides**, the closed loop structures fastened to the fly-rod shaft that hold the fly line on the rod's length.

Roll—The movement of a fish when it arches up and down from the surface as it feeds.

Run—The fleeing swim a fish makes when it has been hooked and frightened. Also describes a stretch of stream just below a riffle and above the pool.

Salmon fly—An artificial fly used most commonly for Atlantic salmon. Also, in the western United States, refers to a common name given to several larger species of stonefly aquatic insects.

Saltwater—A general term used to describe the fish or fishing in salty oceans, seas, and other similar saltwater areas.

Saltwater fly—An artificial fly that is made principally to be fished in salt water. Its hook must resist salt corrosion.

Selective—Refers to the feeding habits of fish preferring special flies or special presentation of flies.

School—A group of same species of fish swimming together.

Scud—A small shrimplike crustacean or a fly imitating it.

Shoal—A shallow-bottom area in a lake or stream or estuary.

Shoot(-ing)—A term referring to the fly line or shooting line that is pulled out from the force or momentum of the casting power and extended fly line weight.

Shoreline—The area immediately adjacent to the water's edge, along lakes and streams.

Shrimp—A widely distributed, important crustacean and also its fly imitation.

Skater—A design of floating fly that has a very long hackle or hair around the hook to enable it to sit high or skate across the water's surface.

Slack line—When the fly line has little or no tension on it between the fly reel, rod, and the fly.

Slough—A sluggish or nonflowing, narrow, blind-end body of water usually created by a stream changing to a new path or channel. The old channel becomes a slough if water still connects it to the stream.

Smolt—The third stage of development of sea-run salmonoids (trout, salmon, char), usually in lengths of four to ten inches.

Snagguard—A device on a fly that prevents the fly hook from snagging or hanging on various obstacles (rocks, logs, moss, etc.) near or in the fishing water.

Snake guide—A simple two-footed, open wire loop fly-rod guide, designed principally to reduce friction and overall weight and hold the fly line close to the fly-rod shaft. It slightly resembles a semicoiled snake in shape.

Snelled fly—An artificial fly with a short permanent section of gut or monofilament attached to it. On the opposite end is a fixed closed loop to attach the snell to the leader.

Spawn—The act of fish reproduction. Also refers to a mass of fish eggs.

Spawning—The act of reproduction between male (cock) and female (hen) fish.

Spawning runs—The movement of fish or a number of fish from their resident water to a more suitable area to mate and to lay their eggs.

Spillway—The outlet section of a lake where the water flows over a particular section of the dam.

Spinner—The term used to identify the second adult stage (imago) of mayfly aquatic insects. A small shiny metal blade that revolves on a metal wire shaft when pulled through the water to attract a fish to the fly.

Spinning—A method of lure-casting that utilizes a fixed-spool casting reel in which the line spins off as the weighted casting lure pulls it out.

Splice—The joining of two fly-line sections together.

Spook—Scare a fish so much that it stops feeding or swims away and hides.

Spring creek—A stream in which the water originates from the flow of subsurface spring water.

Steelhead—A migrating rainbow trout that lives part of its life in freshwater streams and other parts in saltwater oceans or large freshwater lakes.

Steelhead fly—An artificial sinking fly designed for catching steelhead.

Straightening (fly line or leader)—The removal of coils or twists in the fly line or leader caused by their storage on the fly reel.

Streamer—A subsurface fly that imitates small fish or similarly shaped natural creatures a fish might strike or eat.

Strike—A fish hitting or biting the natural food or artificial fly. The action a fly fisher takes with fly rod and line to set the hook in a fish's mouth.

Stringer—A length of cord, rope, or chain for retaining, keeping alive, and carrying caught fish.

Stripper guide—The first large guide on the butt section of a fly rod above the rod handle. It is designed to reduce friction and enhance line-casting and retrieving.

Stripping—The act of rapidly retrieving a fly and fly line that involves making a series of fast pulls on the fly line with the line hand.

Structure—Describes objects in the water that fish would live near. Used more in lake fishing than in stream fishing.

Studs—Metal protrusions on the soles of wading shoes or boots for improving footing on very slick wet rocks or ice, etc.

Swim—The way a sinking fly moves through the water as it is being fished. It may move like a minnow or a nymph, for example, or simply swim as an attracter.

Synthetic tying materials—Fly-tying materials that are manmade, for example, Orlon, Mylar, and FishHair.

Tackle—A general term covering all equipment used in fly-fishing.

Tag end—The forward end of a leader or tippet.

Tail—The caudal fin of a fish. Also refers to capturing and/or landing a hooked fish by grasping it just in front of its tail. The lower or end (downstream) of a stream pool.

Tailer—A tool for tailing (landing) fish. It has a locking loop on the handle that locks around the fish's tail.

Tailing—A term often used to describe a fish feeding in a position along the bottom in shallow water so that its tail sometimes sticks above the surface of the water.

Tailwater—A stream coming from a large man-made dam.

Tailwater trout—Trout that live in the cold-water stream below manmade dams.

Take—The fish's action in catching food or a fly.

Taper—The shape of a fly line or leader. May also be used in describing fly-rod shape.

Terrestrial insect—Insects that are land-borne air breathers. Included are grasshoppers, crickets, ants, beetles, etc.

Tide—The periodic raising and lowering of water levels in streams, lakes, and oceans due to gravitational forces or releases of impounded waters.

Tie—Describes the making of artificial flies. Also term used to describe forming various line, leader, and fly knots.

Tippet—The small end of a leader or additional section of nylon monofilament tied to the end of the leader.

Tip-top—The fly-rod line guide that is fitted over the rod's tip end.

Treble hook—A fish hook with three bends, barbs, and points joined on a common shank.

Trolling—Fishing a fly or lure by pulling it behind a boat. Less commonly, fishing by wading or walking with the fly dragging in the water behind.

Trout—A group of very popular freshwater gamefish that live in cold, pure water. Includes rainbow trout, golden trout, brown trout, cutthroat trout, brook trout, etc.

Twitch—A small movement given to the fly by using the rod tip or a short fly-line strip.

Vest (fishing vest)—A vestlike garment containing a number of various-size pockets used to carry flies and other fishing accessory items while fly-fishing.

Wading—Walking on the bottom of a stream, lake, or ocean in water no deeper than your chest.

Waders—Waterproof combination of shoes and pants used for wading.

Wading shoes—Shoes used over stocking-foot waders for wading.

Wading staff—A walking cane used to assist in wading, particularly on slick, irregular bottoms and in swift water.

Warm-water fish—Fish that thrive best in water temperature ranges from 65° to 85°.

Water clarity—The degree of transparency water has, how far below the surface you can see an object.

Water color—Refers to a water's color tint. It is affected by suspended particles and the bottom color reflection.

Water condition—A general expression fly fishers use to describe the combination of level, temperature, and clarity.

Weedguard—A simple wire or nylon device on a fly that prevents it from hooking vegetation in the fishing area.

Wiggle nymph—A two-section hinge-bodied artificial nymph fly.

Wind knot—A simple but troublesome overhand knot that is accidentally tied on the fly line or leader while casting.

Woolly worm—A design of sinking fly that has a fuzzy or woolly body and hackle spiraled around and over the body's length. Also the larva of terrestrial moths or butterflies.